Aaron,

Imagine what you might do to change the world. Believe for a moment that you can and then... act on that belief.

Peace · Freedom · Equality · Hope

Caryn West
2009

The Trouble with the Alphabet

Through The Eyes Of Innocence

Written and Illustrated by Caryn West

Poetry and Essays:
Caryn West

Graphic Design and Page Layout:
Caryn West

Published and Distributed by:
The Trouble with the Alphabet, LLC
www.TheTroublewiththeAlphabet.com

Artwork Reproduction and Color Management:
Nathaniel Coalson
www.NatCoalson.com

Printed by:
Intelligencer Printing Company
Lancaster, PA
www.IntellPrinting.com

ISBN 10:0-9796850-3-6
ISBN 13:978-0-9796850-3-3

First Printing, 2008

Printed in the USA

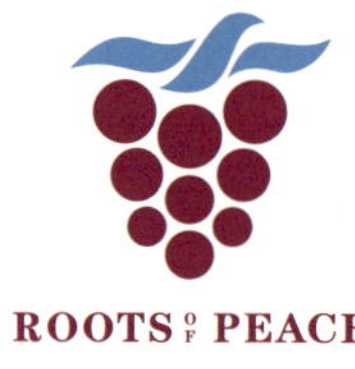

Roots of Peace:
The Trouble with the Alphabet, in association with Roots of Peace, will plant two trees for each tree used in the manufacturing of this book. Roots of Peace is an internationally renowned humanitarian organization dedicated to eradicating land mines worldwide and converting war-torn lands into productive farms and wildlife habitats.

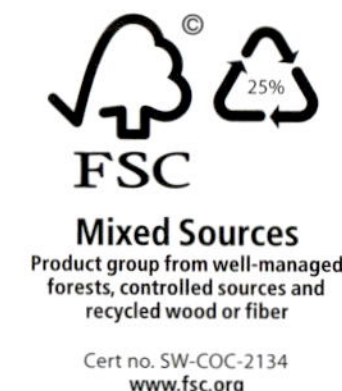

Forest Stewardship Council:
Products carrying the FSC label are independently certified to assure consumers that they come from forests that are managed to meet the social, economic and ecological needs of present and future generations. Additionally all the printed pages of this book are made with recycled paper containing 25% post-consumer waste.

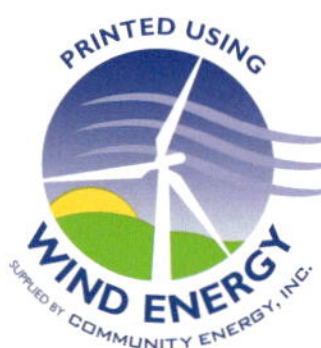

Wind Energy:
Wind Energy is a clean source of electricity produced when specially designed **wind turbines** capture the wind to generate electricity. Like historical windmills, modern wind turbines generate power from the wind. New wind turbines are the fastest growing and most cost-effective renewable energy technology in the world, and are producing power all across the United States.

Colophon

Typeset in Adobe Myriad, Minion, Papyrus and DeVinne Ornaments Regular.

Printed using Pantone® Hexachrome® and High Definition Printing™.

Special Thanks

Mom, I spent the first part of my life with you so I want to thank you first. You never gave up on me and my dreams, even when I failed and needed you to lift me back up. Thank you for everything you've done…You've done so much.

Brock, my husband, my biggest fan and my best friend, we've been through a lot. Thank you for all your help researching, contacting NGOs, communicating with photographers and doing whatever it took to help me make this happen. I couldn't have done this without you. I love you.

Felicia, my beautiful daughter, I know this was a hard time for you and I put a lot of responsibilities on your shoulders. Thank you for understanding and hanging in there with me.

Blaze and Cruz, my special little men, our home is not for the faint of heart with the level of noise and chaos, but when I go to bed at night I thank God I get to wake up being your mother.

Doug, you barely knew me, yet you chose to help me bring this project to fruition. I don't know what to say except that I hope my boys grow up to be men with similar qualities: compassion, generosity, and the desire to support and empower women. Thank you so much.

Nat, I know we had some bumps, but we did it. Thanks for all the technical support.

Kathy, David and every teacher out there, who has or is dedicating their lives to educating the children of our world, thank you.

Dawn, my children love you, and I love you, thanks for all your help.

Caryn West

Table of Countries

Foreword

THROUGHOUT HISTORY, we have looked to artists for inspiration. Their images awaken and stir us, help us to remember, and sometimes surprise us with their honesty. Their unspoken communication can give us compassion when apathy rides hard and reigns over justice. Caryn's work is in this eternal tradition.

The Trouble with the Alphabet reminds us of those who survive with dignity and decency under severe conditions, brutal people and unjust governments. The book even dares to say that one person has the power to make a difference. It spurs the individual to consider that someone who is free can help the un-free; that someone here can help someone there; a reach around the world that lifts and inspires both ends. Albert Camus spoke of the coalition between 'those who receive the lash and those who count it'. This coalition is the target of Caryn's efforts. Each page moves the reader into action that benefits both the doer and the receiver.

In this book, children, always the first to be hurt and harmed in any conflict, receive the full attention their innocence deserves. Talent, paint and prose become compelling instruments that Caryn uses in an unforgettable manner. The combination of the three lifts the veil of detachment and allows us to enter the room where a new day may dawn and convictions are born; convictions that energize and foment new action for decency and justice.

The unnamed and unknown workers; those who give every day within organizations; those who make the tire hit the road; receive their just due in Caryn's call for us to join them. These folks are seldom seen and seldom heard from…but they are there, inside the problem areas doing what they can to help, to solace and be present for the voices stifled in conflict. No heroes, no heroines, just people looking out for the lost, the wounded, the confused, the violated and the hungry.

The children portrayed in this book challenge us to be decent, humane, and just; here for something greater than ourselves. Finally, the book reminds us of the forgotten belief that one need not be rich, powerful or mighty to achieve greatness…it simply takes a step into the light and a belief in justice for all.

The Trouble with the Alphabet is a heartfelt window to the world. It has the power to move the viewer out of indifference and into action. Allow your eyes to be opened and to be filled with the belief that activism does work. Each one of us can make a difference. Collectively we can rewrite the future and in doing so find more happiness in the present.

Take your time. Read carefully and act.

Jack Healey
2008

Called "Mr. Human Rights" by U.S. News and World Report, Jack brought human rights to the global stage by his creative use of media and enlistment of world-class musical talent as advocates and spokespeople. He was named Person of the Week at ABC by Peter Jennings and his music tours of 1986 and 1988 both won 'tour of the year honors' by MTV. He is a humanist in the truest sense of the word and his struggle towards making a better world for all encompasses his life's work. As Executive Director of Amnesty International USA for 12 years, he pioneered new ways to reach youth – the next generation – to deliver the message of human rights.

Author's Preface

WHAT STARTED out as a casual project to paint the alphabet on canvases for my son's room, became a labor of love driven by compassion and a newfound interest in the realities facing children around the globe. As the project evolved it changed my world, or at least how I saw it. The realization that I have a responsibility not just to my own family, but to this life that I have been given, has become my inspiration. The children behind the issues compel me to reach farther, and to work harder. Innocence sacrificed to the mistakes of humanity feeds my creativity, empathy guides my brush and conviction encourages me to put my thoughts to paper. But at the end of the day, it is the hope that I can make a difference that keeps me company when the brush falters and the words get lost in the darkness.

The Trouble with the Alphabet utilizes a fundamental starting point for learning in our society: the alphabet. I have assigned each letter to a country dealing with profound human rights issues and life threatening circumstances. Through the use of art, poetry, and short essays, this book illustrates the many challenges that children throughout the world face each and every day. With that said, it is important to understand that human rights violations, injustices and human suffering occur globally, not just in these countries.

This book is not a revelation of new facts or a handbook for solving global problems. My hope is that it will serve as a catalyst for inciting interest, thought and discussion among those who read it. My belief is that one does not have to be a world traveler with a frequently stamped passport to be aware and compelled to take action. Activism is not confined to being on the ground in one of these countries. Activism is taking action in some manner, wherever you are and with whatever resources you are blessed with or limited by.

This is by no means a children's book in the traditional sense and requires adult supervision, yet I hope that it will instill visionary ideas and promote compassion towards humanity in all people, young and old. *The Trouble with the Alphabet* is a book intended to shake the complacency out of society and replace it with a sense of social responsibility.

Caryn West
2008

Please Note:
The children portrayed in the paintings were selected for the emotions they evoked within the artist. The poetic messages are fictional and do not necessarily reflect the lives or conditions of the children depicted.

The opinions expressed by the author are not necessarily endorsed by the organizations represented within the book.

For more information about a specific entity, the work they do, their unique philosophies and humanitarian approach, please visit the organization's web site.

"Ah, what would the world be to us if the children were no more? We should dread the desert behind us worse than the darkness before."

–Henry Wadsworth Longfellow

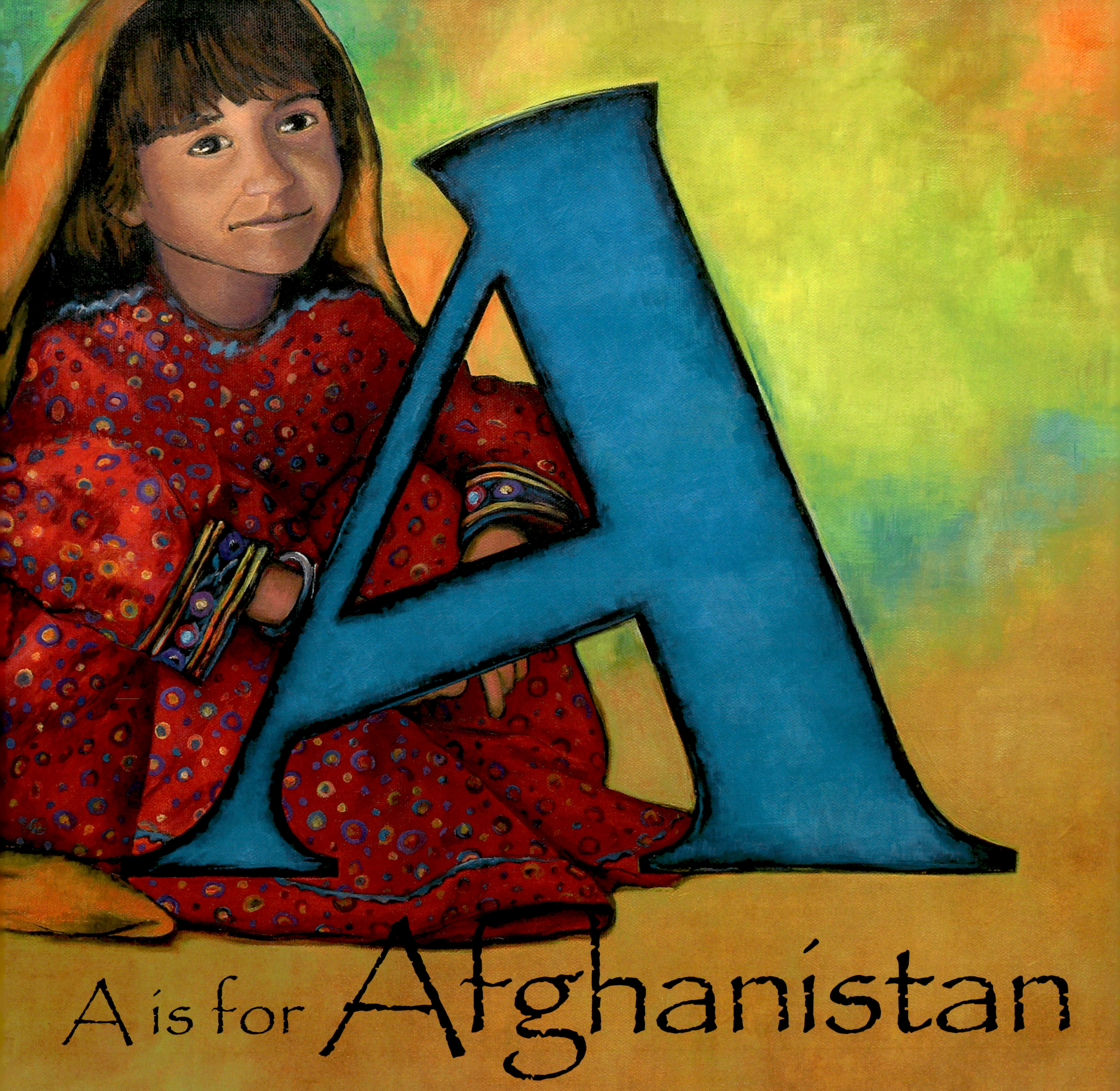
A is for Afghanistan

One Wish

If I had but one wish,
I'd wish that I were free
To learn about the world
And decide what's best for me.

I wouldn't hide my face.
I'd always speak my mind
Proud to be a young girl
Courageous, smart and kind.

If only I could be so free
And my country didn't fight.
If only I could go to school
I'd learn to read and write.

If I had more wishes,
I wouldn't wish for more
Than the freedom to learn,
The key to every door.

"If we are to teach real peace in the world, if we are to carry on a real war against war, we shall have to begin with the children."

–Gandhi, Religious Leader

About "One Wish"

THERE ARE MANY factors that make life difficult and often dangerous for the children of Afghanistan. Extreme poverty, harsh living conditions associated with decades of conflict, and the country's own geography and climate are all culprits. But arguably, it is the long history of oppressive leadership through hard-line groups like the Taliban that has created the greatest challenges.

When the Taliban were ousted from power, many believed it was the beginning of a new climate in which freedom, equality and human rights would finally be realized. The world assumed that through a host of strategies, proposals, projects and the support of many countries working together to improve the lives of the Afghanistan people, success was imminent. Although some progress has been made, the situation today is considered a grave humanitarian crisis.

The Taliban remain an oppressive presence in Afghanistan. Continued conflict between Taliban insurgents and multinational forces has resulted in a spike in security issues. There has been an increase in suicide bombings and the attacks on schools continue unabated, leaving the children of Afghanistan in perpetual turmoil. The Taliban have always been against education for the women of Afghanistan. Losing their seat of power did nothing to squelch this opposition. Today they use fear tactics, such as "night letters" to threaten both teachers and parents; these letters imply students will be harmed, even killed. Imagine if the simple act of walking to school carried with it the possibility of falling under gunfire. This is a grim reality for the children in many parts of Afghanistan. In the first six months of 2007, forty-four schools were attacked. Schools for girls and girls themselves are often the targets, making education a dangerous dream. Currently, about half of Afghanistan's primary school-age children are not enrolled. Unless security improves, this number will rise.

Afghanistan is also considered one of the most dangerous countries in the world in which to give birth. An alarming number of women die during childbirth, and the child mortality rate is exceptionally high. According to the United Nations, one in four Afghan children die before reaching their fifth birthday. Part of the difficulty in addressing these issues is that over forty percent of the country is beyond access or accessible only at great risk of violence and danger. Recovering from three decades of conflict is a difficult task for any country, but when security issues continue to deteriorate and the central government's authority is weakened, new challenges can make or break a country's future. If the current situation is allowed to continue, Afghanistan's children will be left on the brink of catastrophe with a dark future looming ahead. A decaying and under-resourced health system will continue to take the lives of mothers and children, and the progress made in the campaign to educate women and girls will be stalled or reversed.

For a long time the perception has been that the issues in Afghanistan can be dealt with through military efforts. The fact that the children today are at least as vulnerable as they were at any time during the war indicates the need for a new strategy. Health, protection and education need to be the focus of all future efforts. While Afghanistan presents a difficult humanitarian challenge, Afghan children deserve the world's support—our support—to finally bring them out of the darkness.

Did you know… The United Nations has described Afghan women as being "among the worst-off in the world"?

Our Mission

Women for Women International provides women survivors of war, civil strife and other conflicts with the tools and resources to move from crisis and poverty to stability and self-sufficiency, thereby promoting viable civil societies.

We envision a world where no one is abused, poor, illiterate or marginalized; where members of communities have full and equal participation in the processes that ensure their health, well-being and economic independence; and where everyone has the freedom to define the scope of their lives, their futures and to strive to achieve their full potential.
In the last 14 years, we have:

- **served more than 153,000 women**
- **distributed more than $42 million in direct aid and microcredit loans**

How We Do It

Taking control of their destiny

In war, armies use rape and torture to make women feel worthless, unclean and powerless. As a result, many women survivors feel that they have been stripped of their rights. Leadership training and rights awareness education helps women to embrace the fact that yes, they do have rights; yes, they can find their voice; and that yes, they can protect themselves and their children from those who would do them harm.

Rebuilding families, communities and nations

Through our Sponsorship program, women receive direct financial support from a sponsor that helps them purchase the necessities of life – medicine, food, water, clothing and other essentials. These sponsors also form an emotional bond through letter writing that lets these women know that they are not alone.

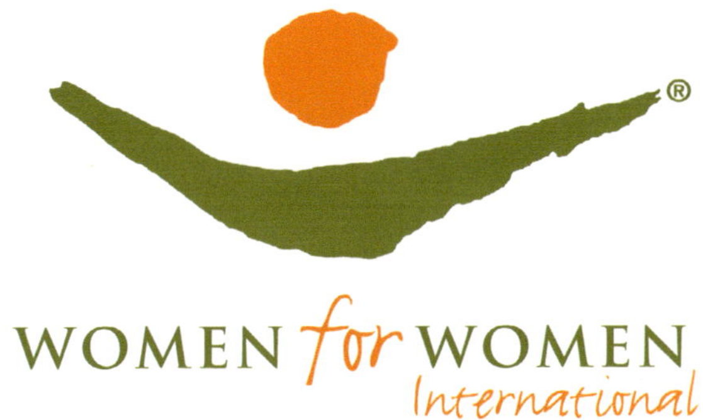

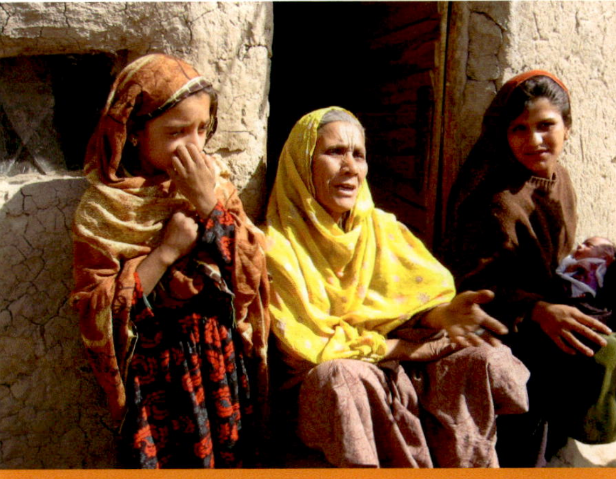

Wherever we may live... wherever our lives may take us...we are sisters, friends, mothers and daughters. It is up to us to change the world, one woman at a time.

A journey toward self-sufficiency

Women for Women International offers job skills training. Comprehensive business services help women start and manage their own micro-enterprises including cooperative ventures that often employ others in their communities. With these new skills in hand, women can then actively participate in the reconstruction of their communities and become active citizens who can help establish lasting peace in their nations.

Helping women around the world not just to live, but to thrive... from victim...

- In Sudan, a woman is more likely to die in childbirth than to graduate primary school.
- After decades of war and Taliban rule, 79% of women and girls in Afghanistan are now illiterate.
- Hundreds of thousands of women in Congo, Rwanda and the Balkans survived rape and sexual violence.

to survivor...to active citizen.

Of our graduates:

- 96% know their rights and can protect themselves and their families from abuse.
- 88% created or sought support networks in their own communities to help them achieve their goals.
- 87% have more income to support their families, send their children to school and invest in the future.

We Believe...
Stronger Women
Build Stronger Nations.

It is essential that we pay attention to what women go through as they live through war and as nations are rebuilt. The women we serve are unseen warriors for humanity. Their weapons are not guns but guts. We have learned that engaging women is the most effective avenue toward creating lasting change and stability within a society. If we can stabilize the women we serve, they can in turn help stabilize their communities and their countries.

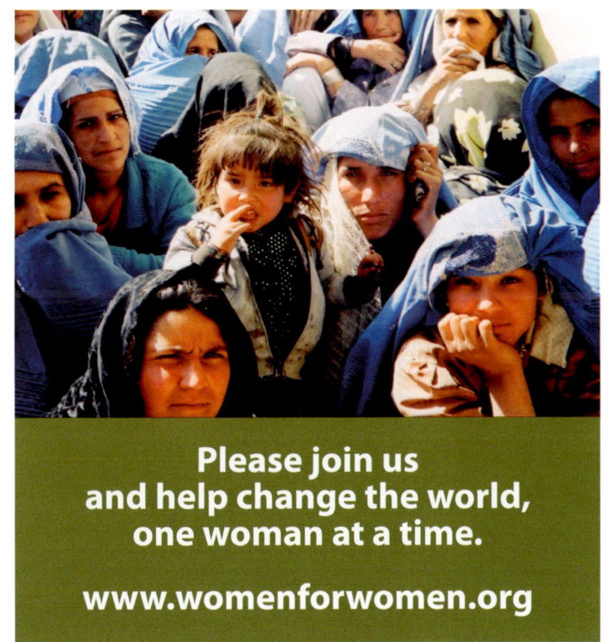

Women for Women International • 4455 Connecticut Ave. NW, Suite 200 • Washington, DC 20008 • www.womenforwomen.org

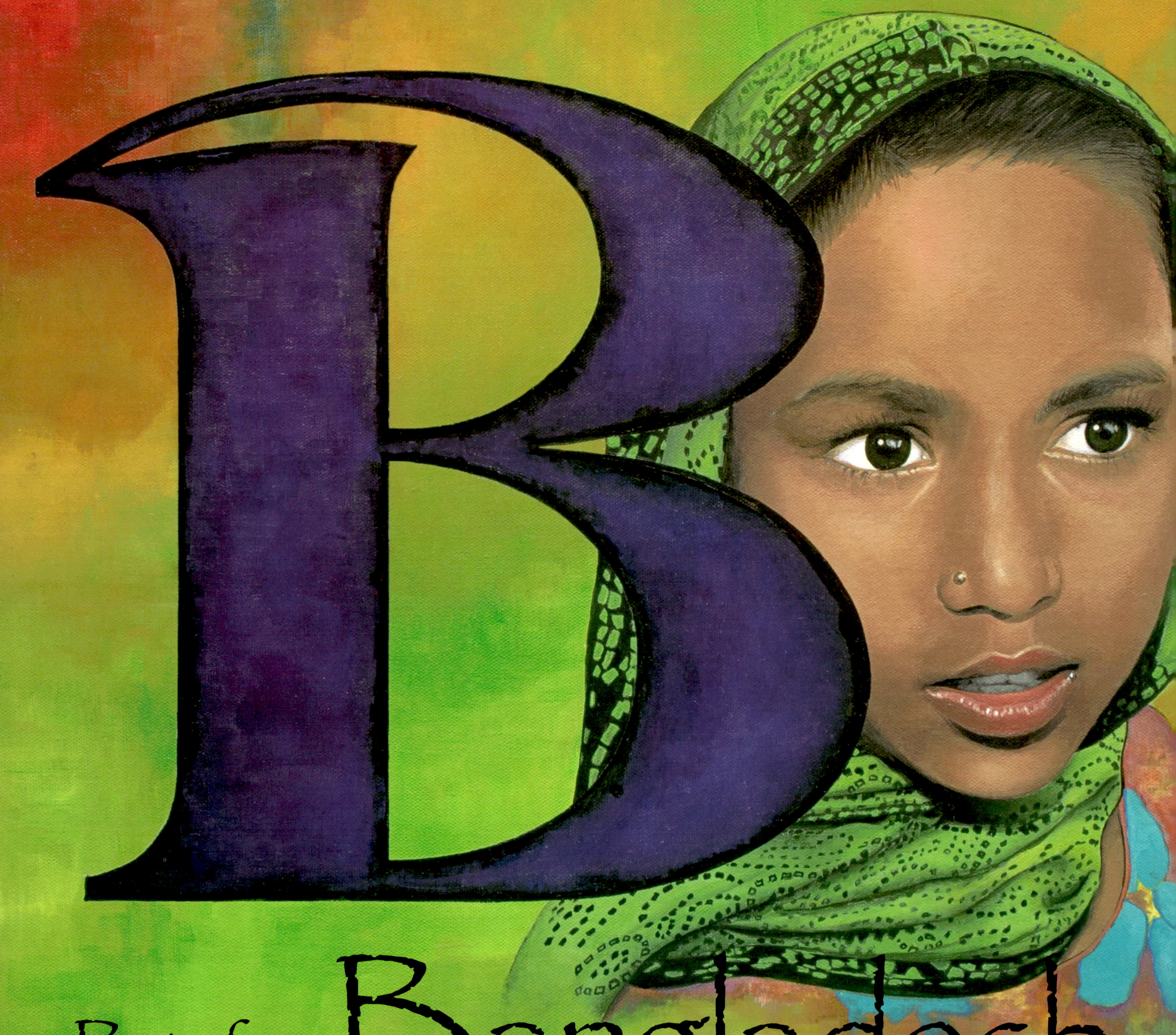

B is for Bangladesh

Because I am a Girl

I think they love my brother more,
Because he is a boy.
I'm not sure they wanted me,
Or that I bring them joy.

It makes me sad to stay at home,
I'd like to be in school.
But they have other plans for me,
Because I am a girl.

I hear them talk of marriage,
As if I have no choice.
Is it because I am a girl,
A child without a voice?

This man they say I'll marry,
I feel nothing for but fear.
Can't they see my sadness,
Whenever he is near?

Is it because I am a girl,
I can't have more from life,
Than being a family servant,
Or becoming an old man's wife?

"A quality education has the power to transform societies in a single generation, provide children with the protection they need from the hazards of poverty, labor exploitation and disease, and give them the knowledge, skills, and confidence to reach their full potential."

–Audrey Hepburn, Actress

About "Because I am a Girl"

IT IS NOT UNCOMMON for a man to secretly hope that his expectant wife will deliver a boy, a tiny copy of himself. Most men are overjoyed when, regardless of the gender, a healthy baby is born. In Bangladesh, this desire for a boy is more than a passing prayer. The arrival of a girl is seldom celebrated, as she is considered a burden, not a gift. Instead of joy, there is grief.

Growing up in Bangladesh, often in the complete absence of love and sense of value, girls are denied many basic rights. They receive medical care inferior to their male siblings, sometimes not at all. They are commonly denied schooling and even receive smaller rations of food. Their health and welfare is generally compromised, resulting in a significantly higher rate of malnutrition among girls than among boys.

Even before reaching maturity, girls in Bangladesh face tremendous pressure from society and their families to marry at a very young age. Sadly, the motivation to marry off a daughter is sometimes nothing more than the perception of one less mouth to feed. For young girls, the consequences of these early marriages can be tragic, sometimes deadly. Girls under fifteen are five times more likely to die during pregnancy or childbirth than girls in their twenties. There is an increased risk of contracting HIV or other sexually transmitted diseases. Additionally, these child brides rarely receive an education and are therefore deprived of any economic opportunities in the future. Widespread and heartbreaking, these underage, forced marriages routinely undermine and destroy the lives of Bangladeshi girls.

In Bangladesh and other countries around the world, gender discrimination is embedded deeply within cultural beliefs, so bringing about change requires a delicate balance of education and support. On the other hand, when the discrimination is fueled by poverty and results in gut wrenching decisions parents feel forced to make, understanding and compassion are critical. Whether culturally driven or the result of desperate circumstances, gender discrimination is a gross violation of rights that we need to address. Without attention to the causes and even greater attention to the need for change, these damaging patterns that exist in places like Bangladesh will repeat themselves again and again, leaving one generation of girls after another powerless and subject to abuse. Girls deserve more opportunities than serving their families or becoming the pawns of men three or four times their age. They deserve the freedom to be children, the right to an education, the time to become women, and the chance to lead a life of their own choosing.

Did you know... Over forty percent of girls in Bangladesh are married before they are fifteen years old?

THE HUNGER PROJECT

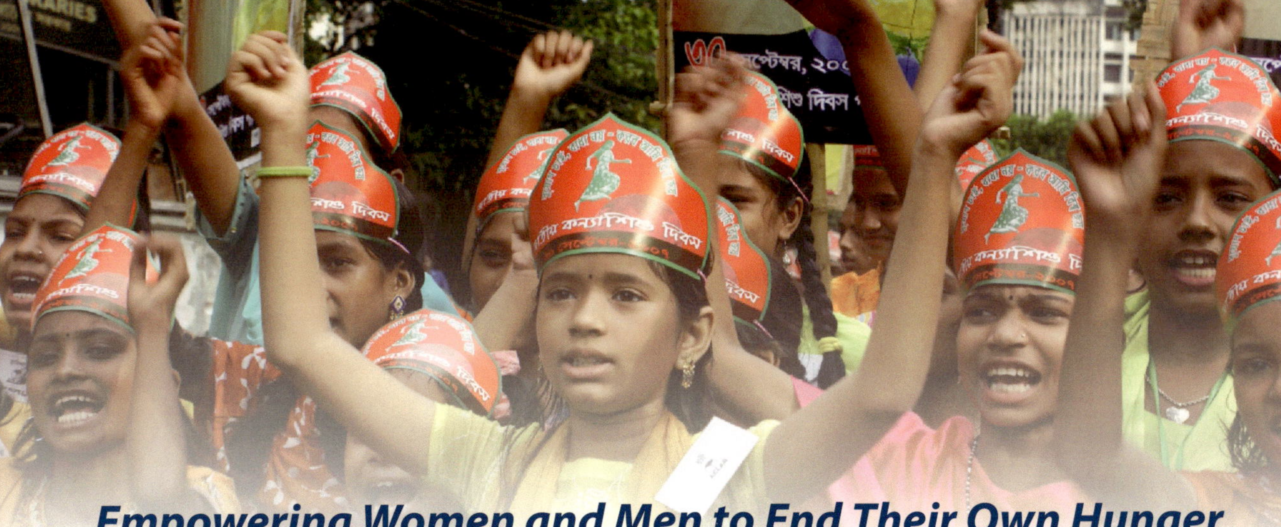

Empowering Women and Men to End Their Own Hunger

Our Mission in Bangladesh

The Hunger Project (THP), a global, strategic organization committed to the sustainable end of world hunger, recognizes that the future of Bangladesh resides in the future of its girls. As long as girls are treated as inferior and less valuable than boys, the general well-being of society in Bangladesh cannot advance. Former secretary general of the United Nations, Kofi Annan, has said: "There is no tool for development more effective than the education of girls. No other policy is as likely to raise economic productivity, lower infant and maternal mortality, improve nutrition and promote health – including helping to prevent the spread of HIV/AIDS."

In accordance with these facts, The Hunger Project has designed a strategy to cause a breakthrough in elevating status of girls in Bangladesh. In 2000, we organized the first National Girl Child Day on September 30th. Working with government ministries, NGOs, women's organizations, schools, and the media we seek to awaken people across Bangladesh to the critical importance of providing better health, education and nutrition to girls as the highest leverage investment for the future of the country.

National Girl Child Day is now celebrated in festivities across the entirety of the country. Hunger Project volunteers take a leadership role to ensure that the National Girl Child Day celebrations reach out to villagers in every district.

Essay contests are held in schools throughout the nation. Both boys and girls win prizes for writing about the importance of better health and education for girls in Bangladeshi society.

In Dhaka, as well as in remote rural areas, organizations rally their constituency to hold teach-ins and marches in support of National Girl Child Day.

National Girl Child day generates powerful media coverage in newspaper, television and radio - educating the public on the critical importance of this issue. The girl child is celebrated for who she is and what she means for the future of Bangladesh.

The Hunger Project has made the empowerment of women its highest priority. Through our work, girls' lives are being improved and the future of humanity is being transformed.

Our Vision for the World

Our vision of the future is not based on everyone achieving a Western-style, high-consumption lifestyle, which is environmentally un-sustainable even for the one billion people who now live it. Nor does it permit one-sixth of the human family to continue to live in abject poverty.

The Hunger Project is committed to transcending this polarity — to creating a future that rejects the inevitability of hunger and recognizes the limitations of a consumerist society.

Achieving the sustainable end of hunger means nothing less than creating a new future for all humanity, a future where:

- every day, every person has enough of the right food to be healthy and productive.
- babies are born healthy and strong, and girl babies are prized as much as boy babies.
- children stay alive, so parents can have smaller families.
- women and girls are full partners in society.
- people have control over their own lives and destinies, and all individuals have a chance to contribute.
- the values of honoring human beings and nature flourish.

The Hunger Project • 5 Union Square West • New York, NY 10003 • www.thp.org

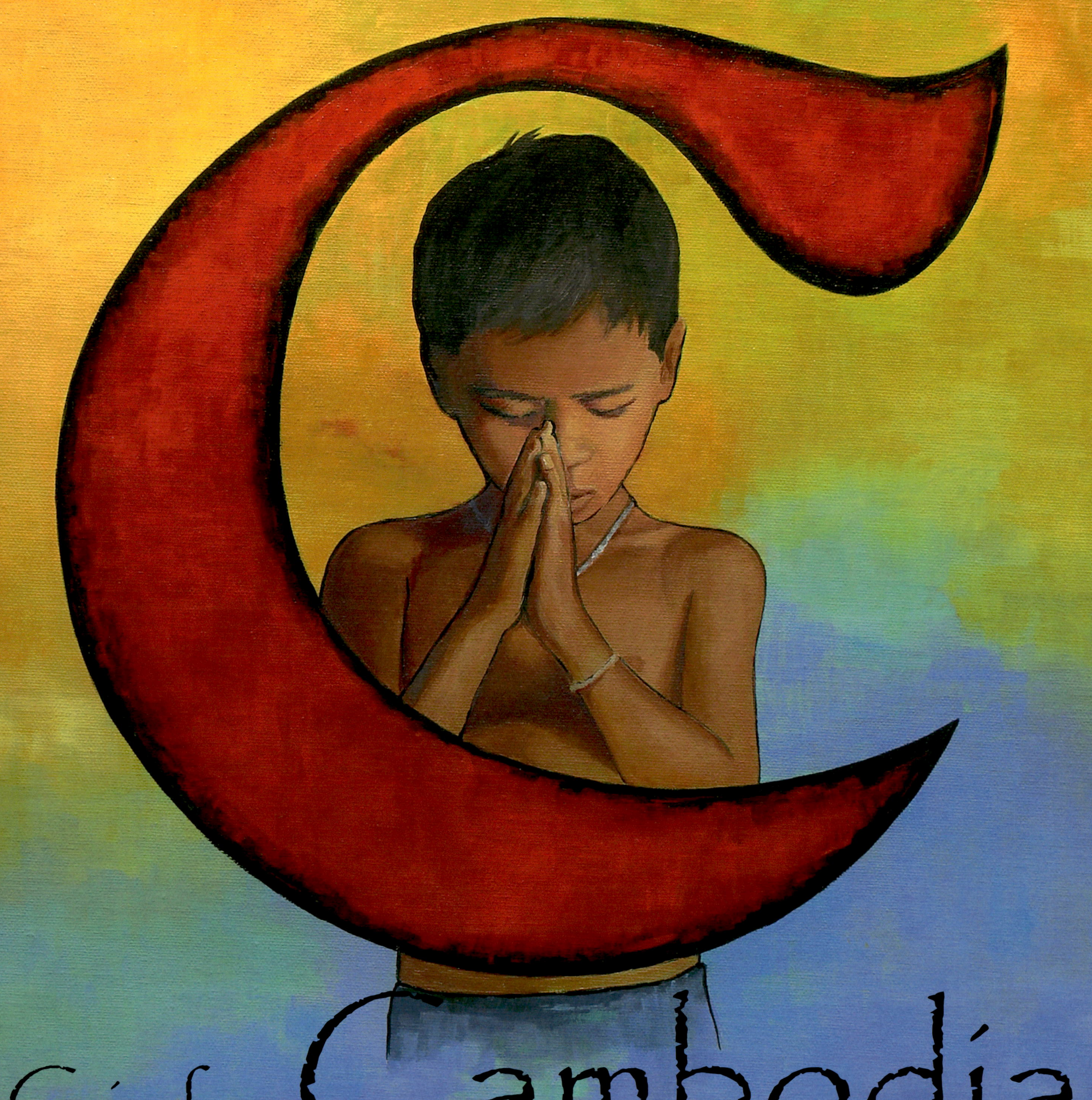

C is for Cambodia

Fear

God, if you're listening,
Please let us know you're there.
We fear we've been forgotten
In a world that doesn't care.

We fear that we can't go to school
Or learn to read and write.
We fear we have no parents
To say to us "Goodnight."

We fear hunger and sickness,
And being taken by a stranger.
We fear the many land mines
That put our lives in danger.

We fear the past and future,
Violence, death and pain.
We fear the cracking thunder
That comes with every rain.

But never being wanted
Is by far the greatest fear.
Worse than any darkness
Or noise that we might hear.

God, can you take this fear
And bring us love instead?
Can you put your arms around us
And tuck us into bed?

"Freedom from fear could be said to sum up the whole philosophy of human rights."

–Dag Hammarskjöld, Former Secretary-General of the UN

About "Fear"

ONE MADMAN, who conducted a reign of terror lasting three years, eight months and twenty days, left behind a legacy of injustice in Cambodia, a legacy born from one of the most shameful periods in world history. During Pol Pot's regime, 1975-1979, it is estimated that between one and three million people died from execution, disease and systematic starvation.

The people of Cambodia were murdered for such "crimes" as being intelligent, speaking another language, wearing glasses or simply having an opinion. Their lives were taken brutally. They were beaten with machetes, axes and clubs, tortured and slowly starved because bullets were more valued than people. Unfortunately, this evil did not die with the fall of the Khmer Rouge, the ruling party during Pol Pot's regime. Nor did it die with Pol Pot, a madman never brought to justice. This evil emerged again in Rwanda and the world watched. Today it is thriving in places like Sudan and Uganda…and we watch.

While the past cannot be changed, it is troubling to be part of a world that can stand by again and again and watch history repeat itself. Where was the rest of the world when these mass murders, torture and starvation were taking place? Why didn't anyone intercede on behalf of these people?

Cambodia has yet to recover. Many believe that the very concept of love was killed along with approximately one-third of Cambodia's population during Pol Pot's rule. Natural resources were squandered and destroyed. The land was left littered with land mines, making it almost worthless to those who survived. Today the world still waits for the International Criminal Tribunal to bring justice to the Cambodian people by prosecuting the surviving perpetrators of these crimes. Isn't time running out for justice? These crimes were committed over twenty-eight years ago. Pol Pot has since died peacefully in his sleep with a self-proclaimed "clean conscience," and many of the other likely defendants are over seventy years of age. While a Tribunal might be important in sending a message to the world, what's more important is the rehabilitation of a country left in ruin. The future of Cambodia's children should not be held in jeopardy while the world waits for a tribunal to deal with the sins of the previous generation.

With growing numbers living on the streets, the family structure compromised and in many cases destroyed due to the country's tumultuous history, the children of Cambodia are tragically vulnerable. Human trafficking, exploitation, poverty, lack of access to education and abuses of basic human rights are at the core of everyday life. The current ruler, Hun Sen, demonstrates an alarming and transparent disregard for humanity with the gross violations taking place in Cambodia today. While we cannot undo the past, we can at least pay more attention to the present. We can try to prevent future mass atrocities by using our voices and putting pressure on our governments. We can become advocates and support policy change where it is needed. Most importantly, we can take care of the children, help them to understand yesterday, keep them safe today and give them hope for tomorrow.

Did you know… During Pol Pot's rule, the Khmer Rouge systematically turned schools into places of execution and murder?

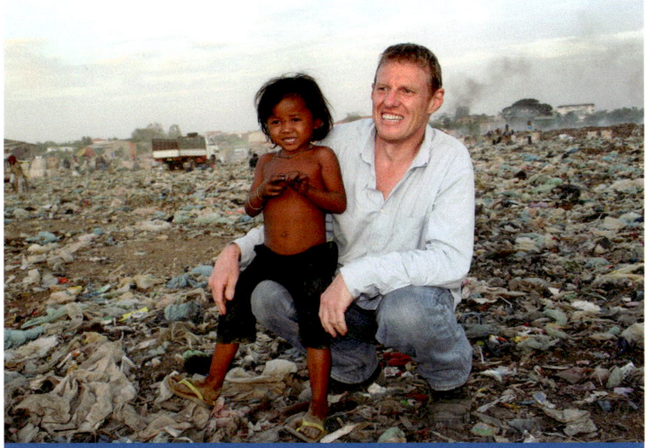

The Cambodian Children's Fund was founded in 2003 by Scott Neeson, then a film executive in Hollywood. In 2004 Scott gave up his career to run the CCF full time and now lives year-round in Phnom Penh.

The CCF was originally developed to provide a safe haven for 45 children in critical need and today cares for over 300 children across three main centers with comprehensive programs and dedicated staff. We are consistently expanding our reach to provide desperately needed services and support to the poorest and most vulnerable communities.

Over two-thirds of our children come from Steung Meanchey, Phnom Penh's notorious garbage dump, where they worked picking through acres of garbage for recyclable items to sell. Many were abandoned by their parents; others came from rural families that were driven from their farmlands by extreme poverty and debt.

Without schooling, healthcare or access to basic public services, these children have little hope of escaping a life of destitution. They are exposed to hazardous work and appalling living conditions. Many are also at tremendous risk of abuse, exploitation, trafficking and prostitution.

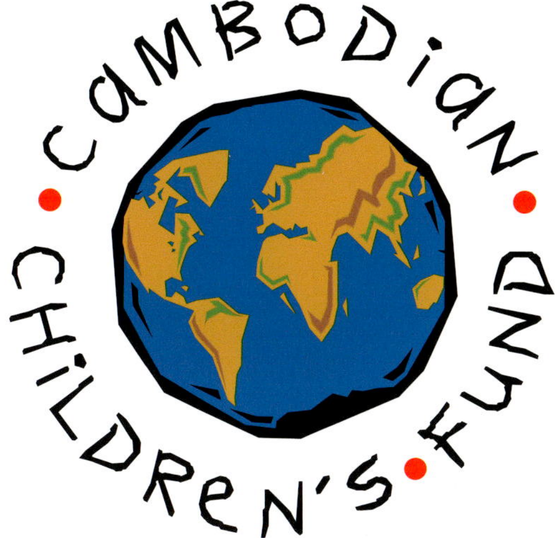

Cambodian Children's Fund

Helping Cambodia's Most Vulnerable Children

"When I first arrived, I felt like I was starting a new life. Before I came here, I was like a flower that nobody cared to water and never saw the sun. Nobody cared or paid any attention to me. But now this same flower is taken to a new place where it can get water and care every day. I can feel the breeze and see the sun."

–Charam, age 10

(from the film Small Voices: The Stories of Cambodia's Children-*A Documentary Film by Heather Connell)*

Dedicated Programs and Activities

By providing optimum education, health care, job placement, technology training and leadership development, these children will enter Cambodian society with the skills, ambition and integrity to become progressive leaders and spokespeople for the emerging generation.

Comprehensive Education

We have three residential education centers providing dynamic academic content modeled on leading US, Australian and British education sources. The CCF's own comprehensive education program includes intensive English, computer studies, mathematics, art and sports, as well as traditional dance, drama and music. Students are also integrated into the Cambodian public school system via special 'catch up' programs.

Health Care & Nutrition

We are actively committed to ensuring each child's optimal health. We treat health problems and nutritional deficiencies as well as provide vaccinations, regular monitoring and high-standard treatment.

Vocational Training

We give our students essential skills, job placements and the confidence to enter the work environment. Areas include cosmetology, computer maintenance, bread-making, graphic design, restaurant management and bio-fuel product development.

Community Outreach

With the addition of the CCF Community Center, centrally located in Steung Meanchey, we now have a focal point for providing basic services such as health and hygiene, food relief, clean drinking water, home repairs, sanitation and job placements to this impoverished urban community.

Building for the Future

As the CCF expands, we are extending our services and resources to the most vulnerable children and their communities, and improving the quality of our programs. We recently opened the Sumner M. Redstone Children's Center, a fourth facility that will care for up to 100 children. The new CCF Community Center Day Care provides early childhood care and education for 2-6-year-olds, and we are also increasing our vocational training programs and planning job orientation for older students

How can I help?

Donations and fundraisers from generous individuals are the lifeblood of our organization. Our sponsorship program is a wonderful way to support and get to know one special child. Partnerships with donors, corporate sponsors and foundations can fund operations or special projects. For comprehensive information visit us online.

The Cambodian Children's Fund • 10801 National Blvd., Suite 560 • Los Angeles, CA 90064 • www.cambodianchildrensfund.org

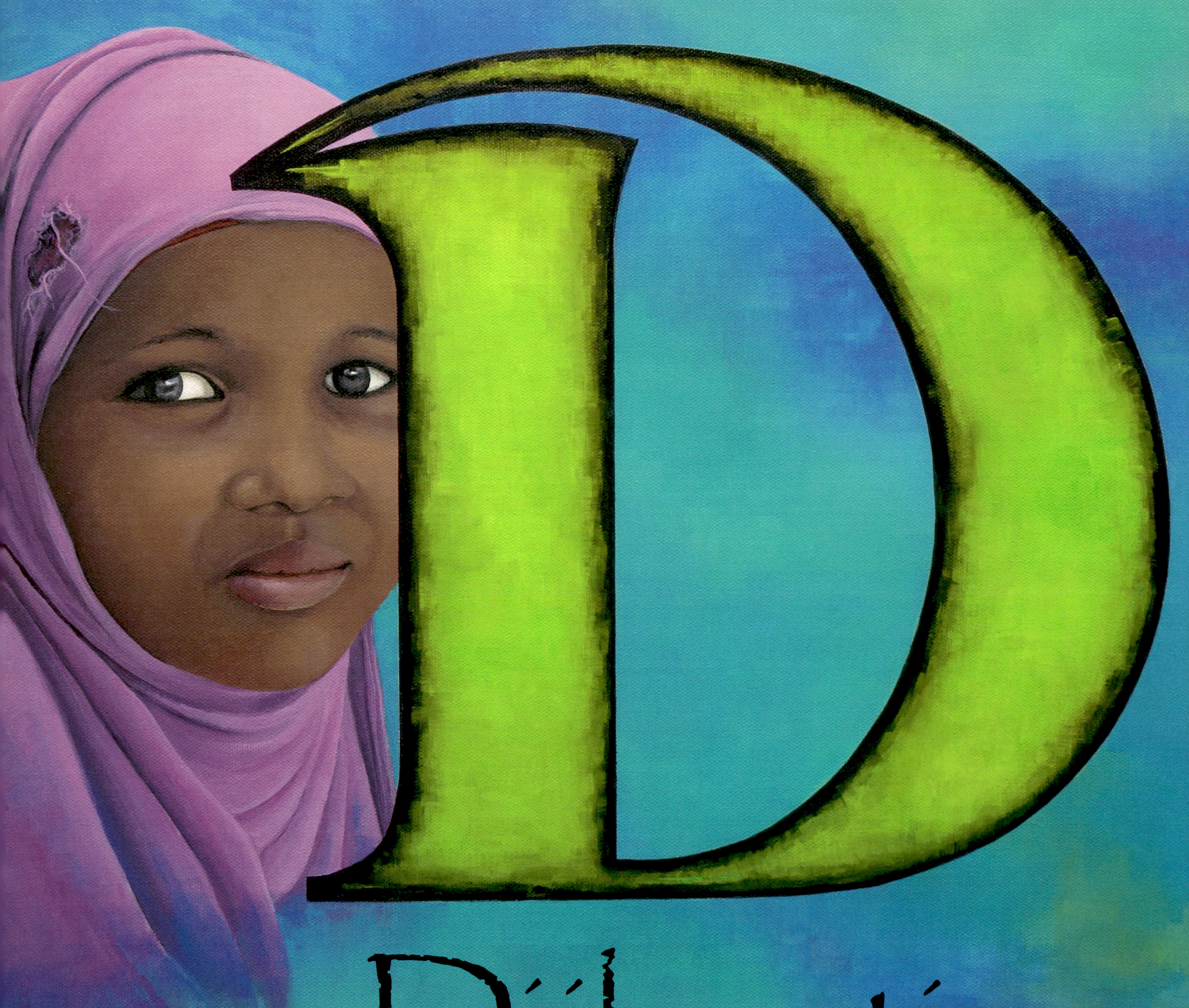

D is for Djibouti

It's Hard

My baby sister is very sick.
They say she won't survive.
They call it malnutrition.
It preys on little lives.

We give her everything we can.
I wish that we had more.
She is three years old today.
They say she won't reach four.

It's hard to feel so helpless.

It's hard to watch her die.

It's hard to watch my mama
Trying not to cry.

"The fact is that this generation–yours, my generation…we're the first generation that can look at poverty and disease, look across the ocean to Africa and say with a straight face, we can be the first to end this sort of stupid extreme poverty, where in the world of plenty, a child can die for lack of food in its belly."

–Bono, Musician and Activist

About "It's Hard"

LIFE IN DJIBOUTI, whether living in the city slums or remote villages, is a challenge that most of us cannot fathom. Simply staying alive can be difficult when even the most basic needs are often out of reach. Especially vulnerable are children under the age of five who become easy victims of malnutrition. Currently, malnutrition is considered a silent emergency in this semi desert country of about six hundred and fifty thousand people. In the past decade, droughts have been more frequent with recovery periods shorter, creating a devastating domino effect within the region. Without a single perennial stream in the entire country, rain is essential to fill water catchments. In recent history, this much needed rain has been insufficient, and the water sources have become critically depleted. Without water, livestock suffers, milk production dwindles, water borne diseases spread and ultimately children die.

Djibouti is considered a disaster prone, low-income, food-deficit country (LIFDC), where sixty percent of the people live below the poverty line, and seventy percent are unemployed. The scarcity of water, along with very limited medical resources, causes a debilitating impact on health and nutrition. Also affected are the educational opportunities for many children. Fetching water has become a critical and demanding chore for children, who must forfeit school to assume this responsibility. In some places, these children must travel as many as thirty kilometers daily to get clean water. In the many areas where clean water isn't available, people have no choice but to use contaminated water, putting the health of entire communities at risk. Without access to medicine or basic health care, even common and curable illnesses can result in death. Without clean water and adequate food supplies, malnutrition continues to prey on little lives. Relief organizations are simply without enough resources to tackle the problem and there is a growing fear that the situation will worsen in the coming years.

The plague of malnutrition among younger children is not new to Djibouti. Yet the significant increase in cases in the past five years is indicative of a "forgotten emergency." With so many humanitarian crises occurring globally, it is easy to forget one small country in Africa struggling to nourish its youngest citizens. We need to remember that what pours from our faucets so easily, what fills our pantries to their limits, and the basic medical care many of us take for granted… could save lives in a country like Djibouti. Children should not cry from hunger, bellies should not bulge from emptiness, and mothers should not have to sit by helplessly watching their children's lives slip away.

Malnutrition is not an incurable disease. It is the result of poverty, drought and lack of education regarding nutritional needs. It can be prevented; it should not be forgotten or ignored. Every child, regardless of where on the globe they reside, deserves to live far beyond their fifth birthday.

Did you know… It is estimated that approximately one out of every ten children die before they reach age five in Djibouti?

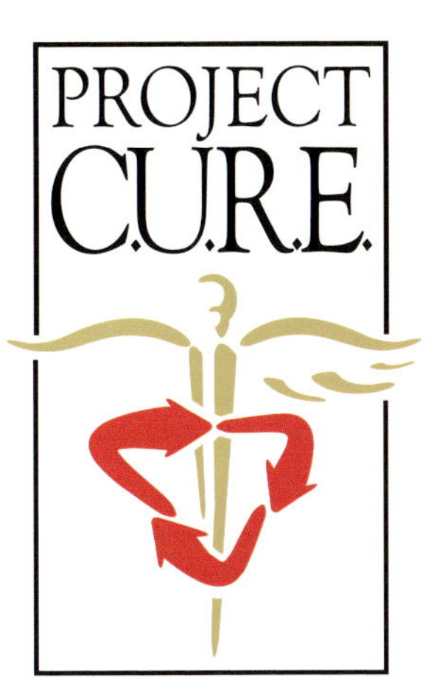

ABOUT PROJECT C.U.R.E.

PROJECT C.U.R.E. is unique among medical aid providers

PROJECT C.U.R.E. was founded in 1987 to help meet the endless need for medical supplies and services in developing countries.

PROJECT C.U.R.E.'s mission is to identify, solicit, collect, sort and deliver medical supplies and services according to the imperative needs of the world. The organization is currently the world's largest distributor of donated medical supplies and equipment to developing nations, working with more than 120 countries worldwide.

PROJECT C.U.R.E. has accumulated an incredible level of expertise in the past 20 years of delivering healthcare around the globe. Since its foundation, trained representatives from the organization have personally visited a large percentage of the world's most austere healthcare facilities in order to ensure that the material donated to the recipient hospitals is appropriate. These representatives also conduct extensive "on-site" appraisals of the capacity of the facility, the character of the recipient and the ability to work through customs. This process ensures that the medical personnel receive the supplies appropriate to the need.

PROJECT C.U.R.E. never charges the recipients for any of the relief shipped and this is made possible by the thousands of volunteers that support the organization's purpose. For every dollar donated to the organization, PROJECT C.U.R.E. delivers an average of $20 worth of medical relief in the form of medical supplies and equipment.

PROJECT C.U.R.E. partners with corporations and donors that pay for the shipping of CARGO containers, which deliver an average of $400,000 (wholesale) worth of medical equipment and supplies to those in need.

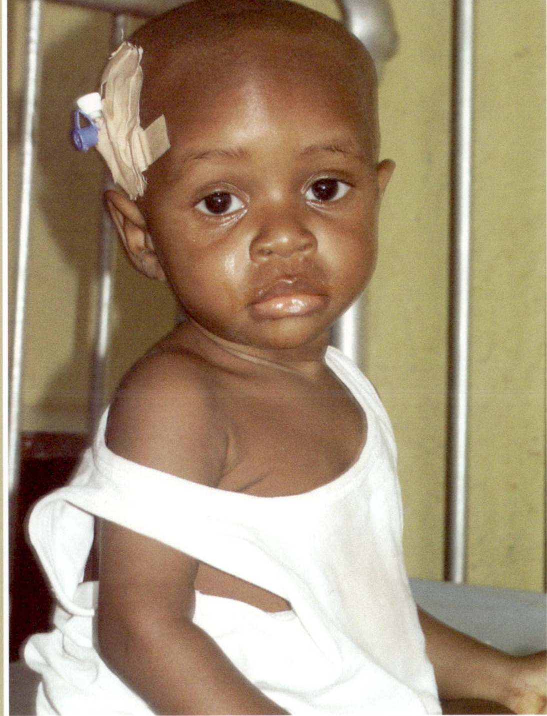

"I don't know what your destiny will be. But this I do know: the only ones among you who will be truly happy are those who have sought and found how to serve others."

– Albert Schweitzer, Nobel Prize Winner

PROJECT C.U.R.E.'s Programs

PROJECT C.U.R.E. has four unique programs that are aimed at helping provide individuals in developing countries with medical relief – ProCURE, CARGO, CLINICS and KITS.

PROJECT C.U.R.E. ProCURE gathers new and overstock medical supplies and working equipment from manufacturers, wholesale suppliers, hospitals, clinics and individuals and delivers that material to clinics and hospitals in developing countries.

PROJECT C.U.R.E.'s CARGO containers are the size of a semi-truck trailer. CARGO provides an average of $400,000 in medical equipment and supplies. Each week PROJECT C.U.R.E. delivers an average of two to three CARGO containers of medical supplies and equipment to hospitals or clinics in developing countries.

C.U.R.E. CLINICS provides an avenue for volunteer medical professionals to travel to developing countries where they offer medical services to people in need. Locations where PROJECT C.U.R.E. has operated CLINICS include: Djibouti, Kenya, Rwanda, Ghana, Bolivia, China, Togo and more.

C.U.R.E. KITS are specially prepared boxes containing essential medical supplies and instruments. C.U.R.E. KITS are designed to meet the needs of short-term medical missions abroad. C.U.R.E. KITS can be hand-carried by an individual or group to hospitals or clinics in developing countries.

Delivering Health & Hope To The World

International Headquarters • 10377 E. Geddes Avenue • Centennial, CO 80112 • www.projectcure.org

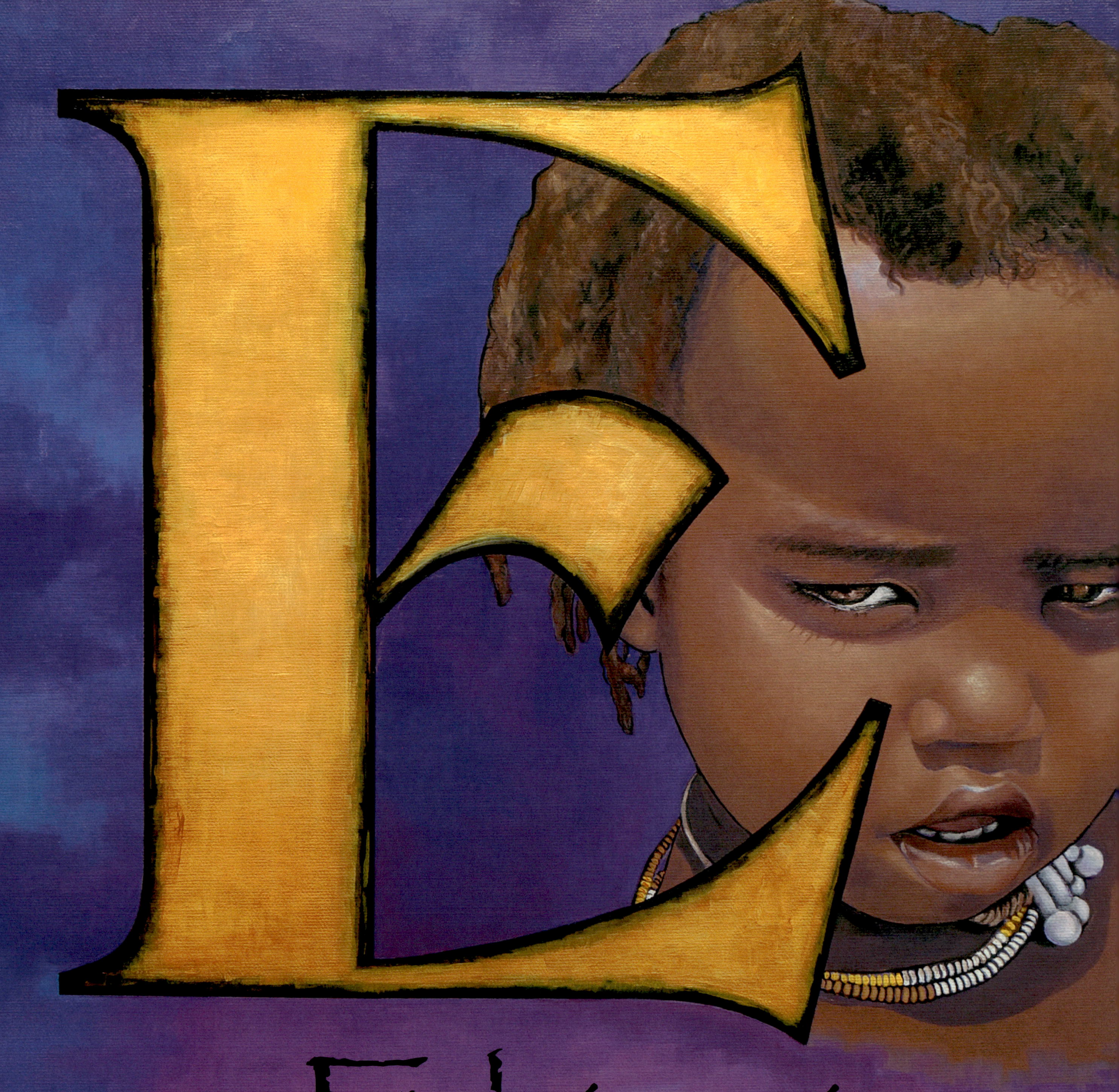

E is for Ethiopia

A Promise

Mommy,
Can you help me?
My mouth is really dry.
I just need a little drink.
I promise not to cry.

You say there is no water.
You say there is no food.
I don't understand,
But I promise to be good.

I'll close my eyes.
I'll go to sleep.
I promise that I'll try.

I am just a little girl.
I do not want to die.

"It is poverty to decide that a child must die so that you can live as you wish."

–Mother Theresa, Humanitarian

About "A Promise"

According to Mestawet Taye Asfaw, an Ethiopian scientist, "'real hunger' has nothing to do with the uncomfortable feeling of an empty stomach for a few hours or even a day. Real hunger is no food in the house, nothing growing in the fields and no money to buy anything. Real hunger is people dying and livestock dying because the drought has left them with nothing, absolutely nothing to eat anywhere."

Ranked as one of the least developed countries in the world, Ethiopia has become an international symbol of famine. With a population of roughly seventy-seven million, over forty-three million Ethiopians do not receive the minimum daily nutritional requirement, resulting in one of the highest rates of malnutrition in the world. Eight out of ten Ethiopians rely on agriculture for their livelihood. Chronic food shortages are part and parcel in a region that has experienced five major droughts in two decades, add to the mix record breaking floods, a shifting political climate, and civil unrest and you have a country in the midst of a humanitarian crisis teetering on the brink of catastrophe. More than three million Ethiopians are in critical need of emergency food aid. These people are more than hungry...they are dying.

The escalating conflict being waged in the Somali region of Ethiopia between the Ethiopian military and the rebel force known as the Ogaden National Liberation Front is only making matters worse. In an attempt to eliminate the ONLF, a group that has been fighting for self-determination for years, the Ethiopian government launched a major military campaign in June 2007. This military action triggered another humanitarian crisis that threatens the well-being of an additional two million people in the surrounding areas. Caught in the fray, innocent and vulnerable families are being subjected to violence, war crimes and rampant human rights abuses including famine caused by food and relief blockades.

In general, Ethiopians are locked in the vortex of a vicious cycle. Before they can recover from one calamity, they are faced with another. In one part of the country drought destroys crops, wipes out entire herds of livestock, and opens the door to famine and disease. In another part of Ethiopia, government and civil conflict erupts into violent expression, wiping out villages and communities, and adding millions to the list of those already in critical need of aid. While most of us are familiar with the perpetual struggle for existence in Ethiopia, many of us are not aware that given the right technology and financing, many of the rivers in Ethiopia could bring water to areas in need. Many people are not aware that some of the finest coffee beans in the world are grown in Ethiopia, nor do they realize that unfair trade practices prevent hard working farmers from feeding their families with the fruits of their labor. Kept at the low end of the bargaining stick in the global market, more and more coffee farmers are forced to grow a more lucrative crop, a drug called Khat, instead.

We know so much, yet we seem to learn so little. Around us, we see computers getting faster and smaller, houses getting bigger and better, children getting more spoiled and people becoming more indifferent to anything that really matters. Meanwhile, across the globe, people are suffering and children are dying...for as little as a single drop of water. It doesn't need to be this way.

Did you know... Less than twenty-two percent of Ethiopia's population has access to a clean water supply and that children sometimes walk up to six hours to collect water?

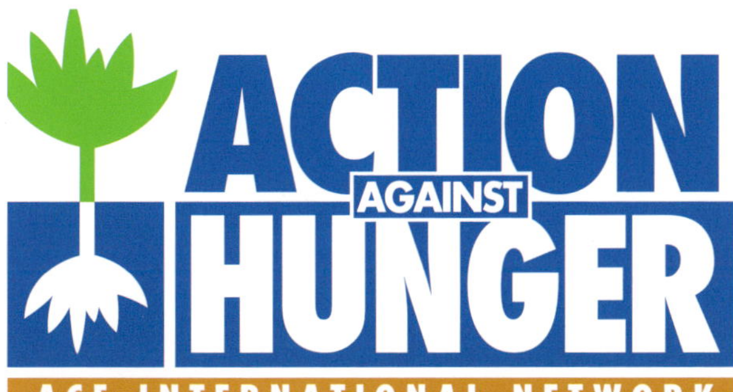

Innovative Solutions for World Hunger

Action Against Hunger / Action Contre la Faim (ACF) is an international network committed to saving the lives of malnourished children and their families while ensuring access to safe water and sustainable solutions to hunger.

Recognized as a world leader in the fight against hunger, Action Against Hunger has pursued its vision of a world without hunger for nearly three decades, combating malnutrition in emergency situations of conflict, natural disaster, and chronic food insecurity. Our staff of 6,000 seasoned professionals work in over 40 countries carrying out innovative, life-saving programs in nutrition, food security, water and sanitation, public health, and advocacy.

We reach some 5 million people each year, restoring dignity, self-sufficiency, and independence to vulnerable populations around the world.

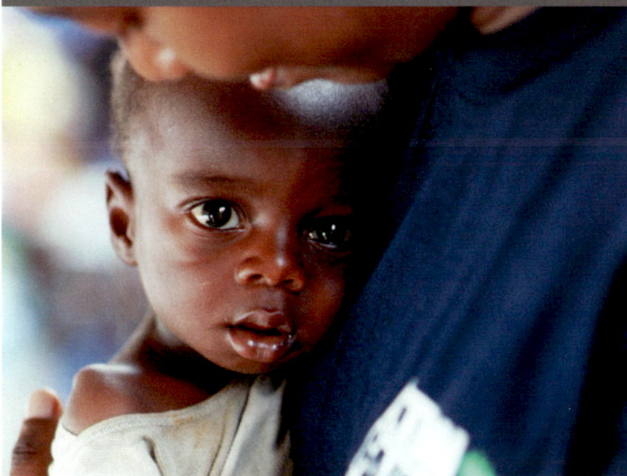

ACF-Congo, Courtesy Burger/Phanie

An Organization You Can Trust

While the programs we run may vary from one country to the next, they all share this defining set of characteristics:

- ***Comprehensive Approach:*** Action Against Hunger integrates activities in emergency nutrition, longer-term food security, water and sanitation, basic health care, and advocacy. To tackle the underlying causes of hunger, we address a range of social, organizational, technical, and resource concerns essential to a community's well-being.

- ***Lasting Solutions:*** Action Against Hunger works to ensure that our programs can be sustained without us. By integrating our programs with local and national systems we transform effective, short-term interventions into sustainable, long-term solutions.

- ***Community-Centered:*** A community-centered approach is central to building local capacity to manage and maintain our programs. Through training, technical workshops, and mentoring, Action Against Hunger builds local capacity and cultivates community know-how.

- ***Independent & Impartial:*** As a nongovernmental humanitarian agency we are apolitical. But when it comes to human suffering, we aren't neutral: We do our utmost to deliver effective humanitarian aid wherever it's most needed.

- ***Full Accountability & Transparency:*** We directly oversee the implementation of our programs, requiring full access to the communities we assist. We are committed to a policy of transparency and disclosure by ensuring that key financial information is publicly available and that our programs undergo external evaluation to assess their impact.

- ***Efficient & Cost-Effective:*** We consistently receive top marks from rating agencies like the Better Business Bureau's Wise Giving Alliance, Charity Navigator (receiving their highest 4-star rating), the American Institute for Philanthropy (top-rated with an "A+"), the Independent Charities of America (as a "Best in America" nonprofit), and Guidestar.

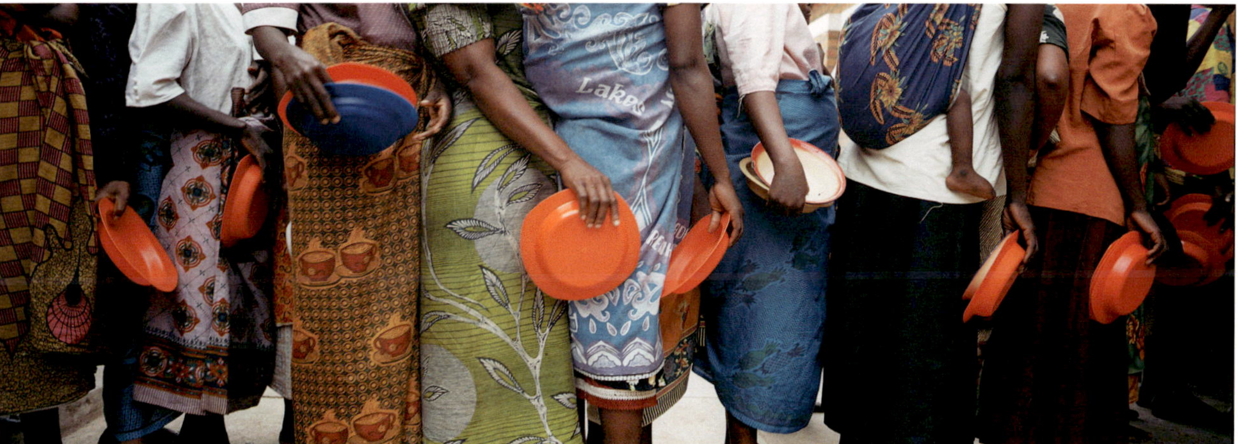

ACF-Malawi, Courtesy M. Atwood/Agence VU

Support Action Against Hunger's Life Saving Programs.
www.actionagainsthunger.org

Action Against Hunger-USA • 247 West 37th Street, 10th Floor • New York, NY 10018 • 212-967-7800

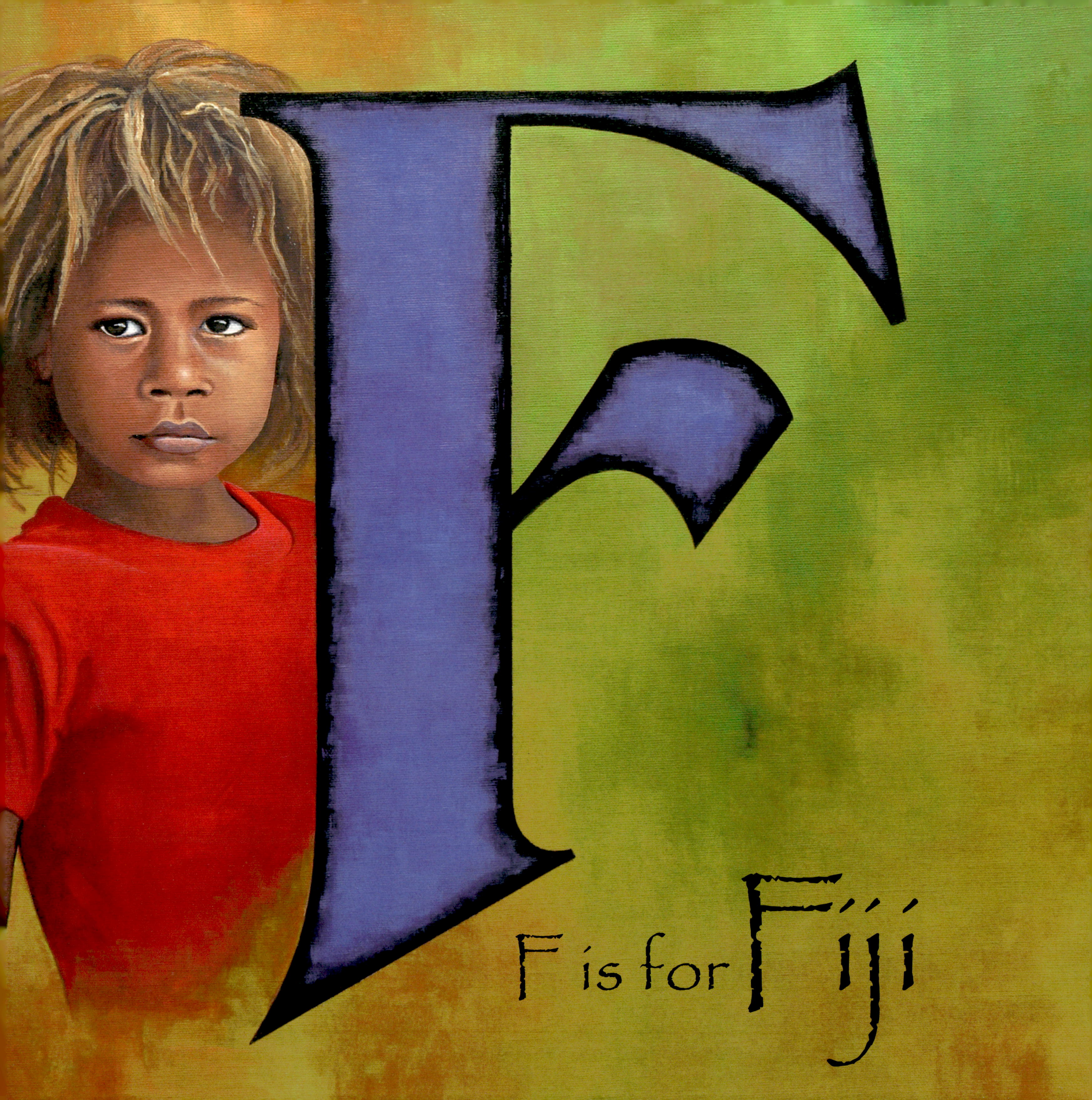
F is for Fiji

The Little Boy

A little boy becomes a man.
This is how it goes.
What the world teaches him
Is likely all he knows.

If he learns about abuse,
Instead of human rights.
What will he hold onto
In the darkness of his nights?

If he watches girls get hurt
Used and thrown away.
If he sees crimes committed
And no one has to pay.

If he learns about the world
From things that don't seem just.
If innocence is sold
For money, greed and lust.

If no one cares enough
To shape his heart and mind.
If he never learns the things
That make us good and kind.

If compassion isn't taught
In every single land,
Who will the little boy be
When he becomes a man?

"Throughout history, it has been the inaction of those who could have acted; the indifference of those who should have known better; the silence of the voice of justice when it mattered most; that has made it possible for evil to exist."

–Haile Selassie, Former Emperor of Ethiopia

About: "The Little Boy"

MANY AN OLD MOVIE romanticizes the Pacific Island region with images of beautiful island girls rowing out to greet the lonely fishermen coming to shore. It's not so romantic when the beautiful girl is a child being traded for fish that her father can sell in the market. Fiji is another perceived island paradise where instead of being raised in an atmosphere of love and morality, children are commonly violated and abused. Old cultural beliefs, distorted to accommodate the needs and desires of men, serve as convenient justification for the young, especially girls, to be denied their most basic human rights.

The Pacific Islands, in general, are critically flawed in the regard, protection and socialization of their children. Children have a very low status in society with girl children falling squarely at the bottom. Raised to view themselves as inferior to males, most Fijian girls grow up with a deeply entrenched sense of powerlessness, leaving them vulnerable to many forms of abuse. Contrary to popular belief, the greatest threat to Fijian girls does not come from the tourists who commonly visit the island seeking sexual encounters with underage boys and girls. While sexual tourism in Fiji is a serious issue, the greater threat comes from within. "Children are most at risk in their own homes and communities and with people they know and trust," according to a recent UN report examining the issue in five Pacific Island countries. The report revealed an alarming predominance of the abuses being perpetrated by male islanders, often relatives and authority figures in the child's life.

The problem is likely much greater than the study revealed. In a culture cloaked in secrecy, most of the abuses against girls go unreported as the shame and embarrassment to the family is of greater concern than a girl's rights. In cases where it is reported, there can be tremendous pressure from the community to drop the charges as the perpetrators are often people of influence. Without laws defining the crime of "statutory rape" in most Pacific Island countries, and because of the low ranking status of girls, the issue of rape is commonly seen as the girl's fault. This cycle of abuse and lack of punishment of the perpetrators instills a damaging perception of right and wrong in children of both sexes. Girls grow up to be victims and, sadly, boys often grow up to commit the crimes they witness.

In most of the Pacific Island region, a girl's value is primarily in her reputation and her potential for a financially beneficial marriage. When this is ruined, her value is gone. As a result, there are few options left to the victims of sexual abuse and many of them turn to prostitution as a means to survive. When the fear of reprisal from her family and community is too great, a pregnant teen will often view suicide as the solution. Few people know that the Pacific Islands have the highest suicide rate in the world.

The issue of violence against children in Fiji and the entire Pacific Island region includes extreme physical punishment as a means of discipline, rape, exploitation, prostitution, child pornography, sex trafficking and child labor. The cost extends far beyond the price paid by each victim as the climate of violence and injustice perpetuates itself, moving many parts of the Pacific backwards in terms of human development. The chief executive officer of Save the Children Fiji, Chandra Shekhar, put it quite simply when he stated, "Children's exposure to violence at home, school, or in the neighborhood, either by observation or by experience, is the single most powerful risk factor for generating violent individuals. It is our duty to protect children from such violent exposure and work towards creating an environment where children feel a sense of safety, happiness and love."

Did you know… In one year, out of thirty-five reported cases of sexual abuse against children in Fiji, thirty-three were committed by a trusted family member?

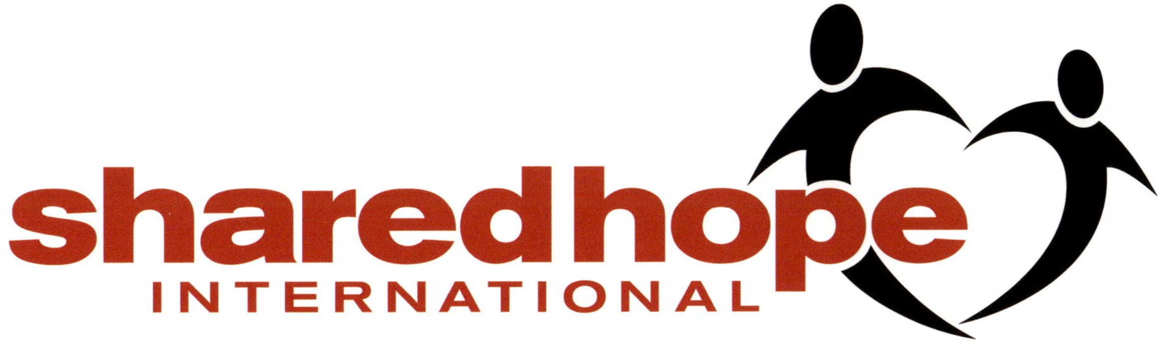

Shared Hope International exists to rescue and restore women and children in crisis. We are leaders in a worldwide effort to prevent and eradicate sex trafficking and slavery through education and public awareness.

How We Started

In the fall of 1998, while still a member of the U.S. Congress, Linda Smith was traveling on Falkland Road in Bombay, India, the location of one of the worst brothels in the world. The hopeless faces of desperate women and children forced into prostitution compelled Linda to found Shared Hope International (SHI), a non-profit organization with the mission of rescuing and restoring victims of sex trafficking.

Our Mission

For almost a decade, Shared Hope International has served the world's most destitute. We have worked diligently across the globe helping hundreds of women and children enslaved in the sex trade. Our three-pronged strategy – prevent, rescue and restore – is producing hope. We're pursuing prosecution of those who prey on women and children and profit from their abuse. We're rescuing victims and giving them a new life, full of hope and purpose! We will not give up. Our objective is clear. We will continue going into the darkness, rescuing and restoring young women and precious children-one life at a time.

Prevent, Rescue, Restore

- ***Prevent*** - SHI has established the first preemptive male driven, demand focused program in America: *The Defenders USA* (www.thedefendersusa.org). We also pursue protection through the training of law enforcement, social service providers, and prosecutors in the U.S. and around the world to ensure proper victim identification and victim-centered responses. Lastley, our *Predator Project* sends qualified investigators to commercial sex markets to document the sex trafficking industry, information which helps strengthen laws and establish better victim services.
- ***Rescue*** - SHI has mobile and stationary medical clinics in the heart of Bombay's infamous red light district where outreach workers intervene in the lives of hundreds of women and children held in sexual slavery, offering them an opportunity to flee the sex industry. In the United Sates, SHI ensures that support exists for victims by working with drop-in centers managed through local partners – many led by survivors of trafficking.
- ***Restore*** - SHI partners with other organizations to care for and nurture victims of sex trafficking in its strategically located *Homes of Hope,* offering medical care, counseling and nutrition. Through our *Women's Investment Network,* we provide educational and vocational training and opportunities to apply those skills.

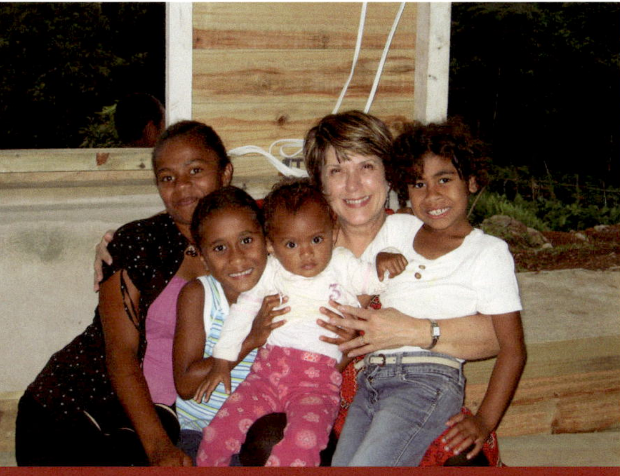

Our Work in Fiji

Home of Hope

Shared Hope International operates a Home of Hope in Fiji. The facility, currently under construction, already cares for 24 women and their children, all victims of sex trafficking. Upon completion, it will be able to house over 200 women and children. In addition to educational and counseling facilities provided, the women are able to gain business training and skills, and build equity for their future through the WIN program which focuses on building and sustaining economic opportunities for women who are victims of sex trafficking.

Giving Opportunity

Providing an Education. Shared Hope is building a schoolhouse at the Home of Hope as a part of the current construction in Fiji. Education, even at the grade school level, costs money in Fiji. With a schoolhouse, we will be able to provide free education for the children of trafficking victims living at the Home of Hope.

Leading a worldwide effort to eradicate the marketplaces of sexual slavery...

One life at a time.

Shared Hope International • PO Box 65337 • Vancouver, WA 98665 • www.sharedhope.org

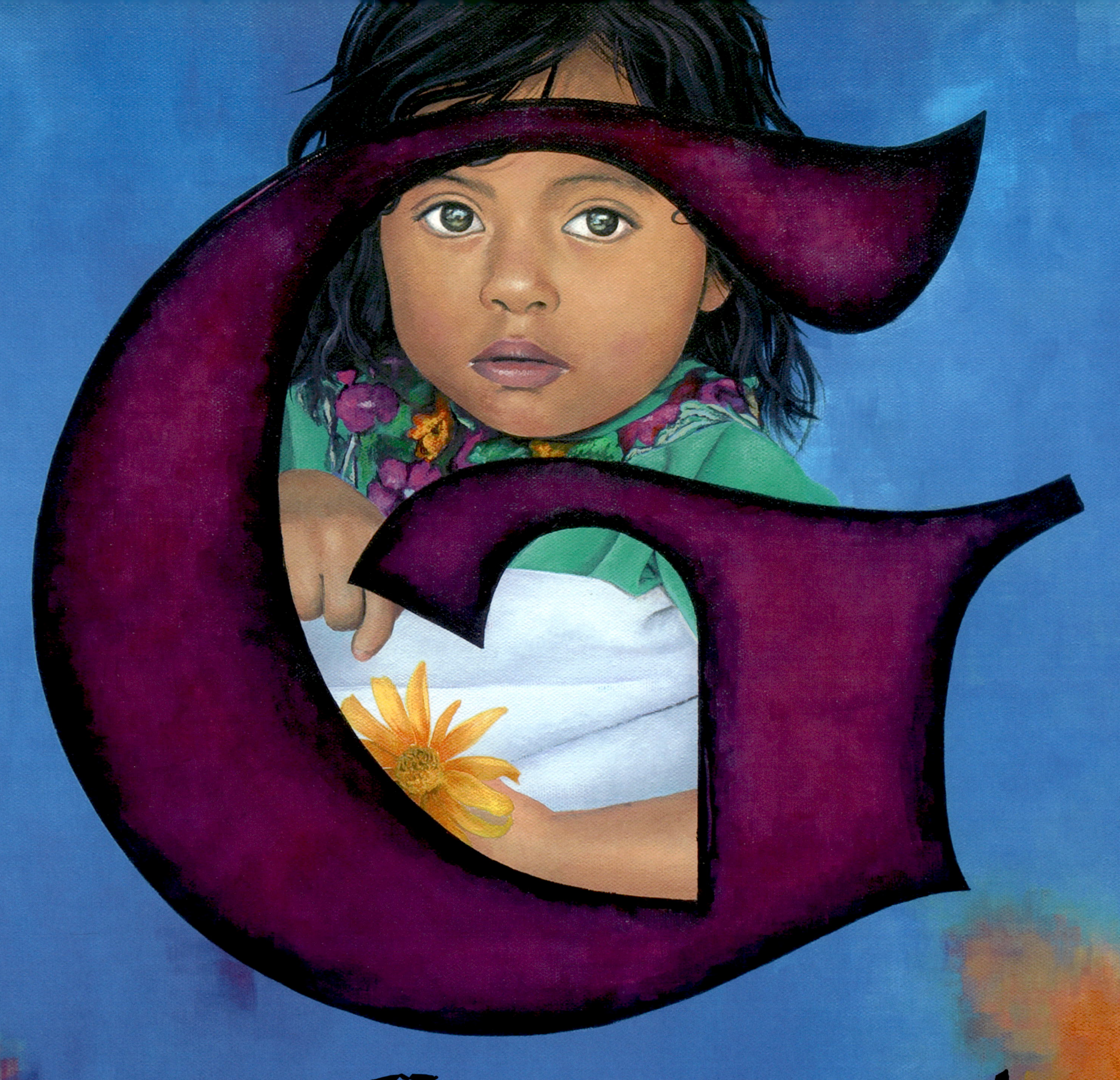

G is for Guatemala

Vulnerability and Violence

Mommy, what's that knife
That you carry by your side?
Why are you so worried
Every time I go outside?

What happened to my sister
On her way to school?
Why'd they have to hurt her?
Why were they so cruel?

I know she isn't coming home.
At night I hear you cry.
Can you help me understand
Why she had to die?

Mommy, I am so afraid.
Please keep me in your sight.
Will you hold onto my hand,
Hold it really tight?

"Children are the seed for peace or violence in the future, depending on how they are cared for and stimulated. Thus, their family and community environment must be sown to grow a fairer and more fraternal world, a world to serve life and hope."

–Zilda Arns Neumann, Pediatrician and Founder of Pastoral da Criança

About "Vulnerability and Violence"

AS CHILDREN, we are usually forbidden to touch knives. As parents, we teach our children how dangerous knives can be. As human beings, we should be appalled to learn that in some countries, children, girls as young as four, walk around with knives or even machetes for their own protection. Where in the world can this be right? Where is it acceptable for children to be left unprotected by both society and law?

Guatemala is one of these places. This is a country that is hauntingly beautiful; breathtaking landscapes, spectacular volcanoes and people as colorful as works of art. Yet, it is also a country that has allowed two of the world's most precious resources, women and children, to be raped, abused and murdered in numbers that are shocking. Equally as shocking, is the lack of action taken on behalf of the victims. According to Sergio Morales, human rights ombudsman, ninety-seven percent of all homicides that occur in Guatemala go unpunished. In his most recent report to Congress, Morales stated that Guatemala has "slid backwards" during 2007, instead of moving forward in its respect for human rights. As evidence he cited the following statistic: on average, sixteen people are murdered each day, among them women and children.

What causes such indifference and the perpetuation of violence, particularly against women and children? Is it rooted in a culture that perceives the male as superior in value and rights, or is it a matter of lawlessness and government corruption which leaves the most vulnerable to be preyed upon? The answer would most certainly be both. Over thirty years of war and unrest, government instability, poverty, drugs and crime all factor into the overall conditions facing the people of Guatemala. Add to this a machismo mentality deeply embedded in the culture, and you have a climate bristling with wariness; where most women and children live as powerless victims, often unaware of their basic human rights. "It is the fashion in this country, in this day and age, to kill women." This is a stunned husband's reaction to the murder of his wife as she walked down the street with her children: the opening scene in *Killer's Paradise*; a documentary about Guatemala's culture of violence and impunity. A seven-year-old was the very first murder victim in 2007. She was raped, murdered and beheaded before being left in plain sight; tragic evidence of a society that has learned to tolerate evil.

Guatemala is a country in need. Its women and children are being murdered, and rarely is anyone held accountable. Because it is not happening to us, doesn't diminish the tragedy. It is happening in our world, and this should be enough to compel every one of us to take action. Pressure from the rest of the world on the Guatemalan government to punish the perpetrators and to protect the vulnerable is critical in bringing about change. Change is essential to creating a better future for the children of this country. The women of Guatemala need to be empowered, their children need to be protected, and their daughters need to be taught that they do have equal value on this earth.

Did you know… Guatemala City has one of the highest murder rates of women in the world?

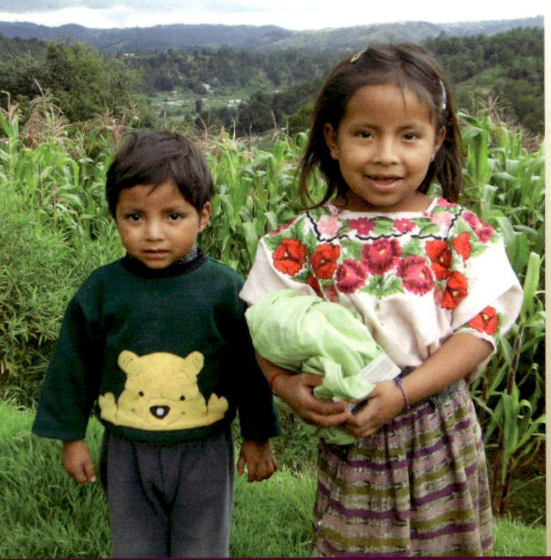

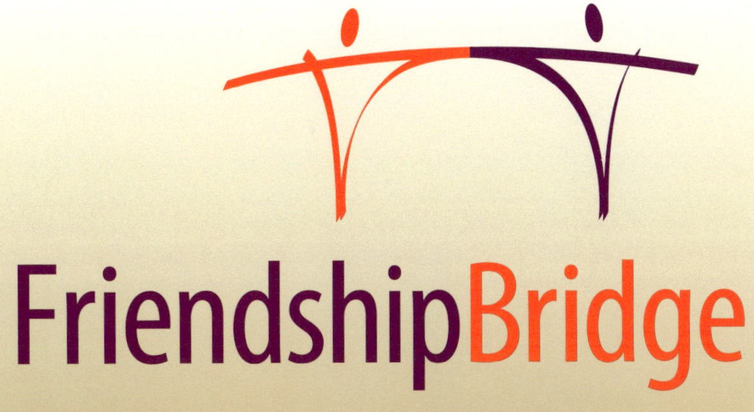

Microcredit programs provide poor families with economic opportunities today, and scholarships for children that secure a brighter future.

In Guatemala, 80% of the arable land is in the hands of 2% of the people. According to a study done at San Carlos University, Guatemala is 1,200,000 housing units short, or in other words, two million people in the country are homeless. 70% of the overall population has had little or no formal education, 38% have no access to health care, and 46% have access but no medicine or cannot afford the medicine that is available.

Friendship Bridge works in rural Guatemala to empower women and their families to create their own solutions to poverty. We do this in three ways:

- Providing small loans to women to start new, or expand existing businesses, that will boost incomes
- Delivering non-formal education to clients in the areas of business development, women's health, leadership, and nutrition, thus empowering them with knowledge that is useful in their daily lives
- Providing scholarships and other school support so their children can attend school

Many women voice the dream of their children getting an education. Our typical loan client has 1.9 years of education. Reading and writing for them is a distant hope, but not for their children. Through education, new and different opportunities will open up that increase the chances of breaking the generational cycle of poverty.

Friendship Bridge is currently providing school support to over 16,000 children throughout rural Guatemala. We are getting kids in school and keeping them in school! This is the best hope for the future of Guatemala.

Why Women? As a group, women are extremely under-capitalized. Women make up 70% of the world's poorest, earn only 10% of the world's income, and own less than 10% of the world's property. Furthermore, women are more likely to use the profits from their business to feed their malnourished families and educate their children.

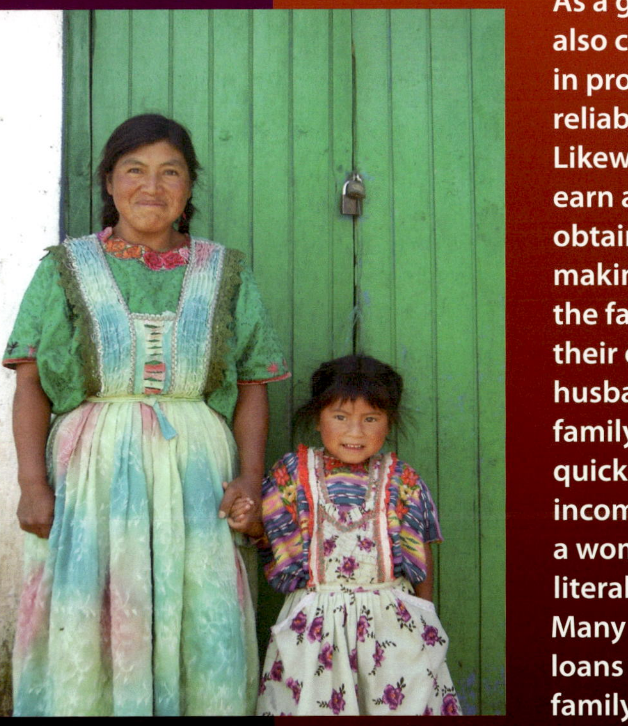

As a group, they are also consistently better in promptness and reliability of repayment. Likewise, when women earn an income, they obtain more decision making power within the family and over their own welfare. Most husbands and other family members are quick to realize that the income generated from a woman's business can, literally, be life saving. Many women use their loans for expanding rural family businesses.

Once women have found their voice, they lead us to their newly awakened dreams for their families and communities.

Friendship Bridge • 3560 Highway 74, Suite B-2 • Evergreen, CO 80439 • www.friendshipbridge.org

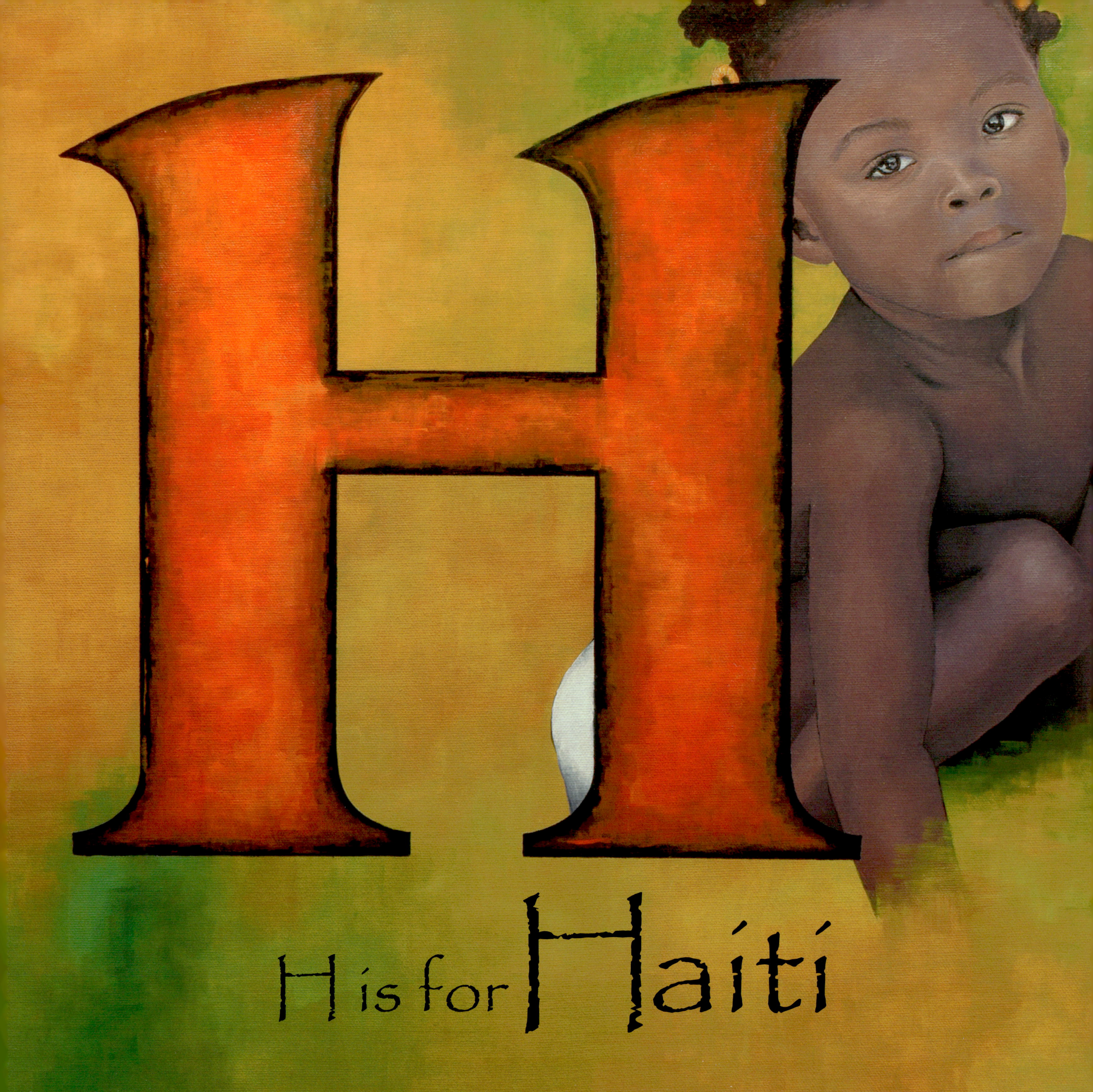
H
H is for Haiti

What I Know

Poverty.
What's it mean?
I'll tell you what I know.

It means,
That we won't go to school,
Like other children do,
Or have clothes to wear
That are clean and new.

It means,
That when we get sick,
No one will make us well,
And if somebody hurts us,
There's no one for us to tell.

It means,
That we might be sold,
Instead of being fed,
Into a life of servitude
Suffering and dread.

It means,
That when I go to bed
Hungry and confused,
I'll wake up the same
Neglected and abused.

"Clean water and health care and school and food and tin roofs and cement floor, all of these things should constitute a set of basics that people must have as birthrights."

–Paul Farmer, Medical Anthropologist and Physician

About "What I Know"

HAITI IS only a three hour plane ride from New York, not a world away like the countries we most often think of when we think of complete poverty and human suffering. With the highest infant and maternal mortality rate in the Western Hemisphere among a slew of other woes, Haiti is the least developed country in the world outside of Africa. Eighty percent of the Haitian population lives in abject poverty, while forty-five percent of the country's wealth is in the hands of one percent of the population. Is it bad luck, bad management or a rampant case of government corruption?

Political scientists refer to Haiti as a "predatory" or "gatekeeper" state; a winner takes all game of politics and corruption; a game that leaves most of the country living outside of a humane existence. A staggering fifty-five percent of Haitians live on less than one dollar a day. Children fall victim to a legal system that incarcerates people as young as five years old for crimes as vague as "associating with bad people." These are usually orphaned or abandoned children struggling to survive in lawless neighborhoods among gangs and thugs. For these children, life is so bad that being locked up, sometimes without hope of release, is safer than freedom.

Where are the people whose job it is to protect the rights of a country's citizens, especially those of children? Instead of security and hope, Haitian society festers with a myriad of self-serving power brokers, violent gangs, drug runners, and a tragically decayed infrastructure. At the very bottom of the ladder, are the children; neglected, uneducated and abused. Half a million Haitian children have lost one or more parents to AIDS or treatable illnesses. Many more have been abandoned by parents who simply could not afford to feed them.

Extreme poverty fuels another of Haiti's greatest demons; child servitude, a practice known in Haiti as "restavec", a Haitian-Creole term meaning "stay with". UNICEF reports that as many as three hundred thousand Haitian children suffer conditions akin to slavery because of an economy that offers parents little or no options. More than seventy percent of these children are girls ranging from three to fifteen years of age. It is difficult to understand how a parent can send their child away to inevitably suffer abuse. In a country such as Haiti and in a culture of dire need, parents often believe that other families with more money can provide their child with better opportunities, education and health care. Unfortunately, the imagined benefits never materialize for these children. Instead, they are treated horrifically, often made to sleep on the floor, under a table, on a pile of rags, or on a piece of dirty cardboard outside. They are forced to do the chores that even the hired help refuse to do, and are commonly beaten for the slightest inadequacy in their performance.

Whether they are victims of almost institutionalized servitude, orphaned, abandoned, neglected or abused, these children are lost in a system that thrives on exploiting the weak; a system where a child who is sick is more apt to be abandoned than cared for, left to die alone, without so much as a hand to hold. It is a system that imprisons children for years, sometimes with little or no cause; a system that allows children to become targets of abuse. The most frustrating aspect of all of this is that the Haitian government appears oblivious to the fact that its own salvation lies in the children it ignores. Almost always more extraordinary than the governments that fail them, children deserve the chance to create a future where success or failure is up to them, not dealt to them by place of birth. Helping the children of Haiti is harvesting the country's greatest potential and hope.

Did you know… Eighty-one percent of Haiti's national population does not get the minimum daily ration of food defined by the World Health Organization?

BEYOND BORDERS

God's Love Doesn't Stop at the Border. Why should ours?

Bringing people together across the rift who want to heal our world.

Our world is divided by many borders – political, economic, cultural, racial, to name only a few. These borders often prevent us from loving our neighbors on the other side of the divide.

Beyond Borders focuses on the division created by the growing economic disparity in our world.

The wealth created in the past four decades through globalization has not been shared equally. In fact, the global gap between rich and poor continues to grow more extreme. Today the poorest fifth of the world's population possesses less than one percent of the world's wealth, while the wealthiest fifth owns more than eighty-six percent. Over 800 million people are chronically hungry while the greatest threat to the health of the world's most privileged is chronic overeating.

This growing disparity is un-sustainable. It is those who are at the extremes of the world's economic continuum, the wealthiest and poorest, who are by far the most destructive to the world's environment. Also, the concentration of wealth breeds resentment and undermines peace at the national and international levels. Beyond being un-sustainable, this disparity is simply unjust.

Jesus identified with the poor, lifted up the poor, brought good news to the poor. Jesus warned the wealthy that their riches imperiled their souls. How should privileged people who claim to follow Jesus respond to poor people who live on the other side of the economic gap?

Children depend on the hope we place in them. We depend on the hope they bring us.

Although the U.S. and Haiti are separated by a flight of less than two hours, the economic distance between them could hardly be greater. Beyond Borders partners with grassroots groups in Haiti to empower people to overcome poverty.

- We work to increase access to quality education.
- We train teachers and community organizers.
- We help small-scale farmers produce more food more sustainably.
- We train human rights advocates to protect children from abuse and bring an end to child slavery in Haiti.
- We host visiting groups and volunteers in Haiti who seek to live alongside and learn to struggle for justice with their Haitian brothers and sisters.

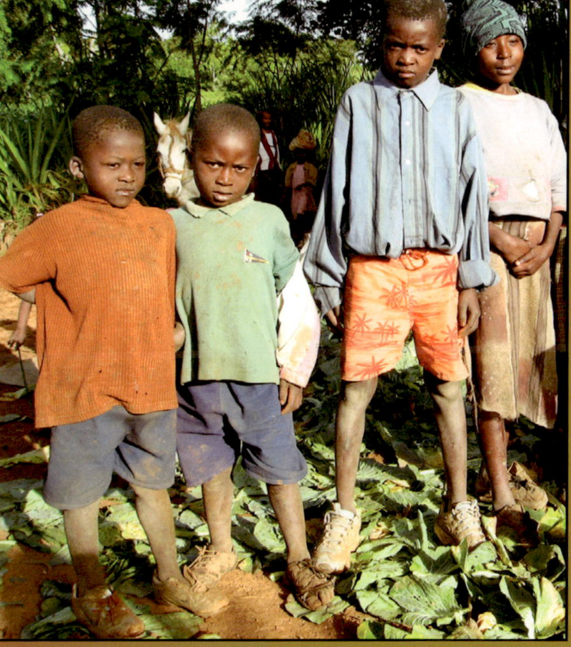

The gap between the neighboring nations of Haiti and the United States mirrors the growing gulf between the privileged and powerless worldwide. It is across this great chasm that Beyond Borders works, building understanding and solidarity between the wealthy and the poor.

Beyond Borders • PO Box 2132 • Norristown, PA 19404 • www.beyondborders.net

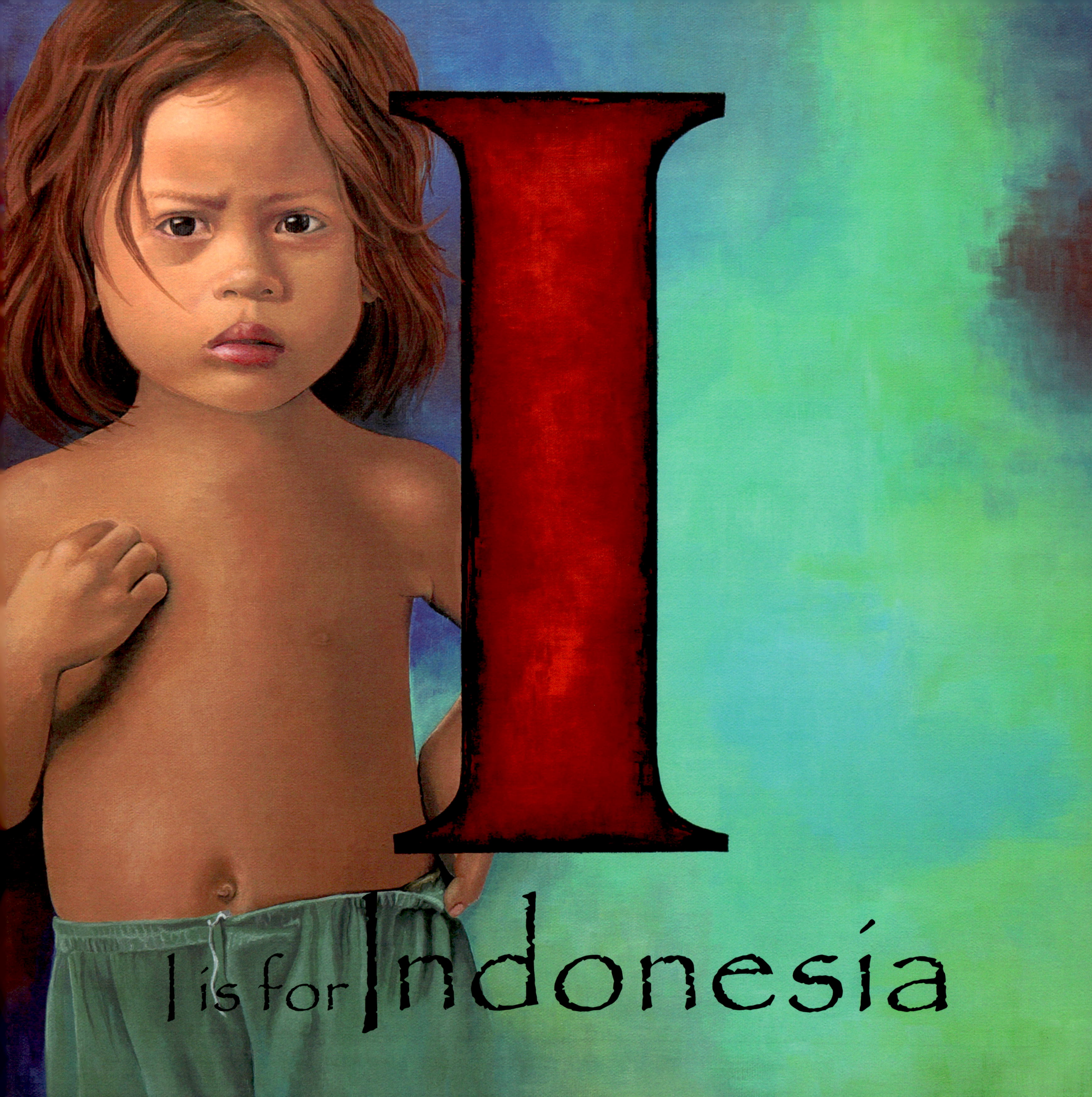
I is for Indonesia

Am I a Burden?

Why do you make me work,
When I am so young?
Can't I just go out and play
And have a little fun?

I am just a child,
It's not my fault we don't have more,
Or that the world is so screwed up
With poverty and war.

Will you give me away,
The way you did my brother?
Will you see me as a burden too,
And sell me to another?

"Children do not constitute anyone's property; they are neither the property of their parents nor even of society. They belong only to their own future freedom."

–Mikhail Bakunin, Anarchist

About "Am I a Burden?"

EVERYWHERE, yet virtually ignored, tiny hands toil and little hearts suffer. Child labor is a plague that eats away at the moral fiber of all humanity. This is not about a little boy delivering papers on his bike, a young girl babysitting her neighbor's child or a teenager doing light household chores. This is about children being forced to work in inhumane conditions; children being mistreated and made to suffer. Child labor is modern day slavery, a vicious undiscerning thief of childhood.

It is estimated that over two hundred and eighteen million children ages five to seventeen are engaged in child labor worldwide. These children are exploited, abused and completely overlooked by society. One hundred and twenty-six million are exposed to dangerous conditions while as many as one hundred and twenty million are working full-time, thereby missing out on an education. If the numbers don't speak to the severity of the situation, they should. These are young children, being treated as slaves, forced to do the work of adults without consideration for their age.

Wherever there is poverty, there are social inequities and potential victims. Child labor is a global epidemic showing no signs of slowing down. Tragically, each one of us without realizing it, plays a role. Our insatiable consumerism, our pursuit of profits achieved through the use of cheap labor, and our tolerance for corruption, foster a climate where evil thrives and children suffer.

Slaving as domestic servants, laboring behind the walls of workshops, hidden from view on plantations; exploited children struggle against all odds. Some work because the economy necessitates it and their culture condones it. Others are abducted by criminals or sold by desperate parents. These are the children that make our shoes, carpets, clothing, furniture, toys, cigarettes, matches, light bulbs, ornaments and jewelry. They dive for our pearls and shells, pack our fish, clean the hulls of oil tankers and work as housekeepers and nannies. They harvest our cotton, rice, sugar, cocoa and coffee. They are forced to work in the sex trade, as street peddlers, pickpockets, in theatre and circus troupes, and even as camel jockeys. The list is endless, the suffering immeasurable.

The Asia Pacific region harbors the largest number of child workers in the world. In Indonesia, which has the world's fourth largest child population, the education system is failing, the government is known for corruption, and child labor goes virtually unnoticed. With half of Indonesia's population living below the poverty line and most struggling to survive on less than two dollars a day, the issue has become an accepted part of life. Adding to the problem is Indonesia's "panscasila" ideology that states that a child's foremost duty is to help their parents. In cultures like these, where the struggle against poverty is the core of everyday life, children pay the price.

We need to stop allowing children to be treated as investments and commodities. We need to eradicate widespread poverty so parents have options other than forcing their children to work or selling them off to traffickers. We need to punish every person who participates in the exploitation or abuse of a child. We need to hold governments accountable and declare corruption unacceptable. We need to understand that laws are only as good as our commitment and willingness to enforce them. And finally, we need to consider the decisions we make in the course of a day and ask ourselves, "Are we living our lives at the expense of a child?"

Did you know… More than one half of Indonesia's two hundred thirty-five million people live on less than two dollars a day?

Since 1951 World Neighbors has helped over 25 million people

WORLD NEIGHBORS

Inspiring People • Strengthening Communities

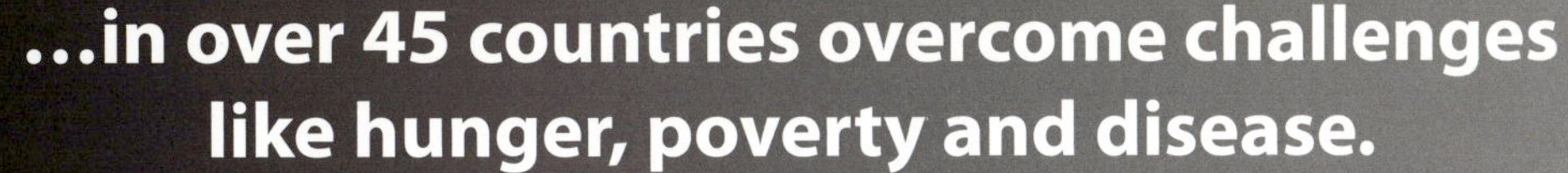

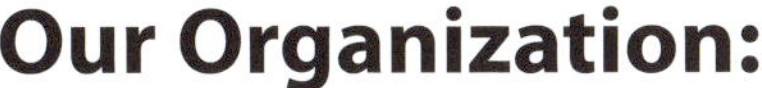

Our Organization:

World Neighbors is an international development organization striving to eliminate hunger, poverty and disease in the most deprived rural villages in Asia, Africa and Latin America. World Neighbors invests in people and their communities by training and inspiring them to create their own life-changing solutions through programs that combine agriculture, literacy, water, health and environmental protection. Since 1951, more than 25 million people in 45 countries have transformed their lives with the support of World Neighbors.

Our Mission:

World Neighbors inspires people and strengthens communities to find lasting solutions to hunger, poverty and disease and to promote a healthy environment.

How You Can Help:

Learn about global issues

- Did you know that 1.3 billion people in the world live on less than $1 a day?
- Did you know that 24% of the people in the world do not have electricity?
- Did you know that 25% of the people in the world do not have access to safe water?
- Did you know that 17% of the people in the world cannot read or write?

Become a global citizen

Did you know that the decisions you make every day impact your global neighbors living around the world? These choices include but are not limited to eating locally grown foods, reducing, reusing and recycling, purchasing fair trade items, etc. We are all connected. We are all World Neighbors.

Support World Neighbors

World Neighbors does not give away food or material aid. Instead, generous donations made by individuals, organizations, corporations and foundations allow us to provide training so that people gain the skills and leadership necessary to work together for long-term, change. Because of how World Neighbors works, one $18 donation will help transform one villager's life for an entire year.

Participate in a World Neighbors service-learning project

World Neighbors offers several service-learning opportunities to engage children, youth, young adults and older adults around the world. The *Art of Trash* project is one example of our service-learning opportunities. The purpose of this project is to allow volunteers to create artwork out of recycled items in order to view trash differently. By having an enjoyable experience with trash, we hope individuals will become better global citizens and learn to reduce, reuse and recycle as we try to decrease the environmental degradation that is negatively impacting World Neighbors villagers living in Bolivia, Burkina Faso, Ecuador, Guatemala, Haiti, Honduras, India, Indonesia, Kenya, Mali, Nepal, Niger, Peru, Tanzania, the Philippines and Timor Leste.

To learn more about this project, please email April Millaway at: amillaway@wn.org

We are World Neighbors
Inspiring People • Strengthening Communities • www.wn.org

World Neighbors • 4127 NW 122nd Street • Oklahoma City, OK 73120 • www.wn.org

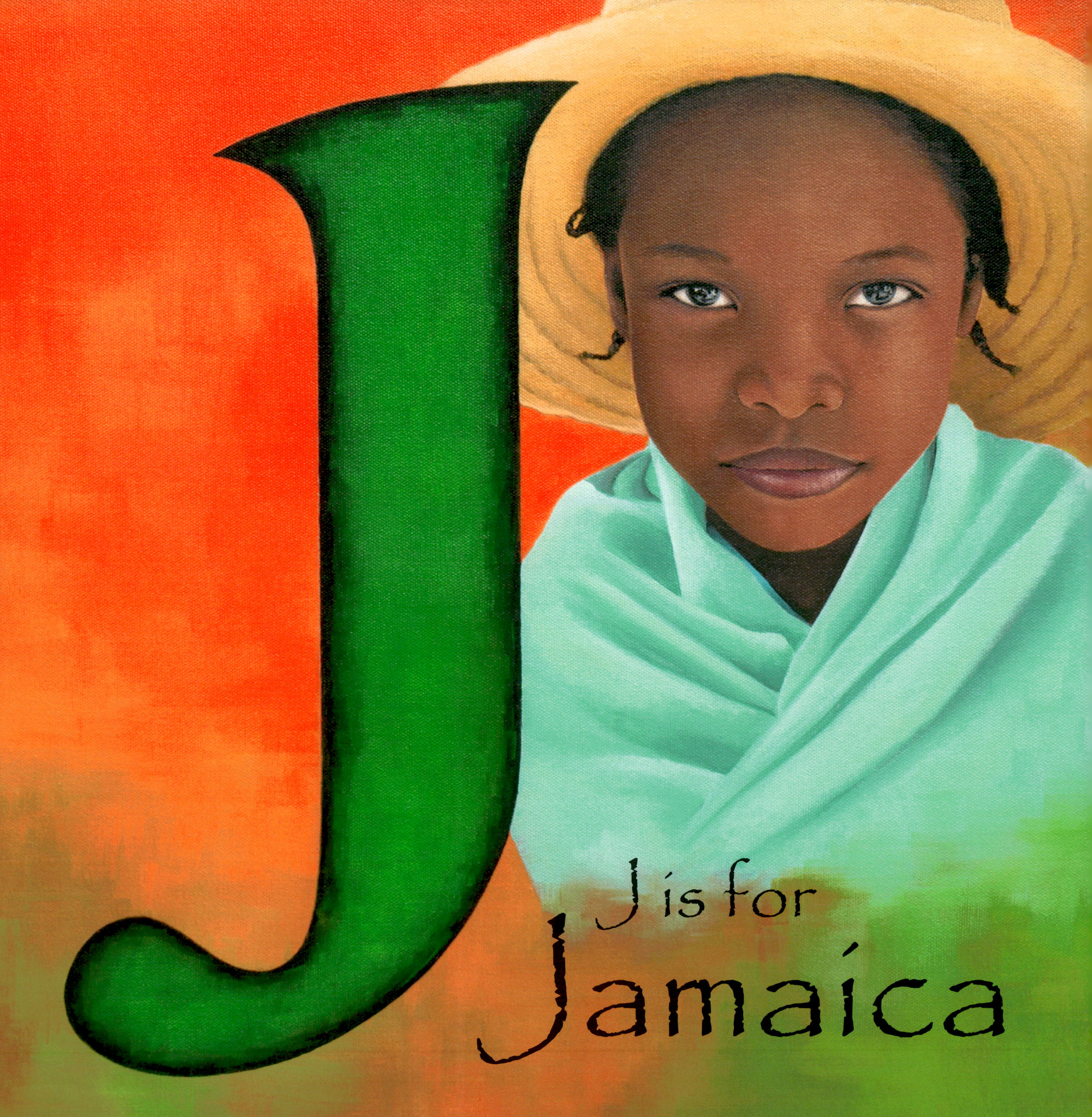
J is for
Jamaica

In Harm's Way

Have you ever been afraid
And wanted to run and hide?
Have you ever been too afraid
To even go outside?

Mommy says the dangers
Are getting worse each day.
She warns me to be careful,
And to stay out of harm's way.

But what does harm look like?
Tell me if you know.
Will it take me while I sleep?
Will it never let me go?

Does it walk along the street?
Will it smile and call my name?
Will it trick me into darkness
By masquerading as a game?

"The conscience of children is formed by the influences that surround them; their notions of good and evil are the result of the moral atmosphere they breathe."

–John Paul Richter, German Novelist

About "In Harm's Way"

MANY OF US think of sand, sun and reggae music when we think of Jamaica. We imagine a carefree respite from the crazy, fast-paced lives most of us are caught up in—a place to relax, enjoy the rhythm of the steel drums and soak up the colorful Caribbean culture. In stark contrast, Jamaica has the highest murder rate in the world. In troubled areas, it is not unusual for the quiet of a tropical night to be shattered by the sound of gunfire, or for children to sleep under their beds to avoid stray bullets.

The illegal drug trade, armed gangs and corruption among law enforcement are common factors plaguing most of the Caribbean Island countries, a shared set of ills that has given the Caribbean the unwelcome distinction as a world leader in violent crime. The statistics are grim. According to a joint UN/World Bank study conducted in 2007, the Caribbean Islands have a murder rate of thirty people per one hundred thousand inhabitants—four times the North American average and fifteen times the West/Central European average. Of thirty-one countries having more than three out of every thousand citizens behind bars, seventeen are in the Caribbean.

In Jamaica, the element of violence is introduced to children at a very young age. Sixty percent of Jamaican children between the ages of nine and seventeen say that members of their families have been victims of violence and thirty-seven percent have had a family member murdered. According to Professor Paulo Sérgio Pinheiro, a global violence expert, "It is common for Jamaican children between ages two and five to be subjected to severe punishment using all forms of violence, boys receiving this punishment more frequently." He adds that while girls are spared more often in regard to this, they are the primary victims of sexual abuse, with girls under sixteen accounting for thirty-two percent of the sexual assaults on the island in 2007. Jamaica is not the carefree world we imagine it to be. Instead, the stakes are tragically high for the children as they are surrounded by violence in their homes, neighborhoods and schools. Many become victims and witnesses of violent crimes and sexual abuse. As a result, it becomes easy for these unprotected and disillusioned children to find themselves following in the footsteps of criminals, gangs and drug dealers.

Lost and powerless in a culture where people have become accustomed to crime, in communities where the police have lost respect and earned distrust, in a system where violence is used to solve all problems, Jamaican children suffer lost childhoods and stolen futures. The scourge of brutal crime casts a dark shadow over this perceived island paradise, yet the vast majority of Jamaicans refuse to accept that this shadow is the future of their nation. In the face of poverty and the ever present threat of violence, they demonstrate courage and hope as they go about their lives, dreaming of a peaceful Jamaica where children are safe and houses don't have bars on every window.

Throughout the Caribbean and around the globe, children are learning exactly what we teach them, and the future will illustrate both our successes and our failures. Violence is not natural. It is not an inevitable part of life that we must live with or die from, and our children deserve freedom from it.

Did you know… In one year, there were an average of four murders a day in Jamaica, of which one hundred and nineteen were children?

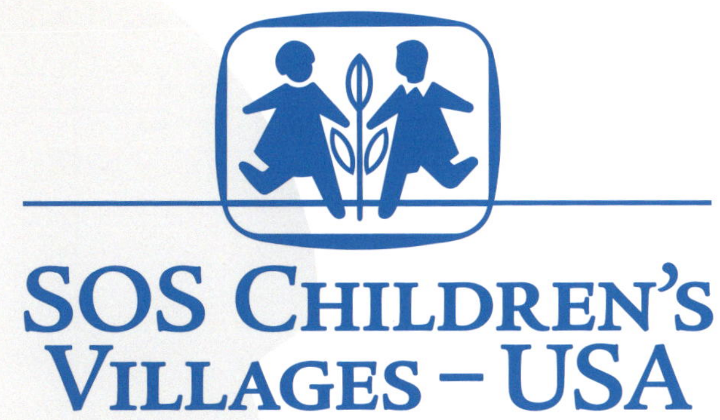

SOS Children's Villages – USA

The world's orphan crisis magnifies poverty, violence and crime

Every child should have the right to grow up in a caring family environment, yet too often this right is denied to the world's youngest citizens. Today, a huge number of children live without parents and hundreds of millions of children suffer from abuse, neglect, exploitation or sheer deprivation as a result of poverty. Children without parental care are easy prey for criminal and terrorist influences.

SOS addresses a crucial problem:

- Over 130 million children have been orphaned in 93 countries worldwide.
- An estimated 25 million children will lose at least one parent to HIV/AIDS by 2010

Economic, structural and political developments impact a family's ability to care for its children. In developing countries, more than one third (37%) of all children are affected by poverty. Malnutrition, poor healthcare and education, all increase the vulnerability of families and decrease their coping mechanisms. Their situation often worsens as community support systems collapse in the face of diminishing state support, the privatization of basic services and rising costs of appropriate child care.

SOS raises orphans in a family and works to prevent child abandonment

SOS Children's Villages has pioneered family-based care, providing support for orphans for nearly 60 years. SOS community outreach programs target at-risk children and their biological families to strengthen their caring and coping mechanisms to prevent child abandonment.

Our Vision

We believe that every child should grow up in a home with love, respect, and security.

SOS Programs contribute to community development:

- 67,000 orphans in over 450 Villages are raised in a family setting
- 467 SOS public schools enroll over 100,000 students annually
- 414 community centers provide social-support programs to over 250,000 people

SOS serves each child and each community. Our schools, vocational training centers and medical facilities are used by local families in need. And our family strengthening programs have a goal to prevent child abandonment by helping young mothers through literacy programs, job training, day care and micro lending.

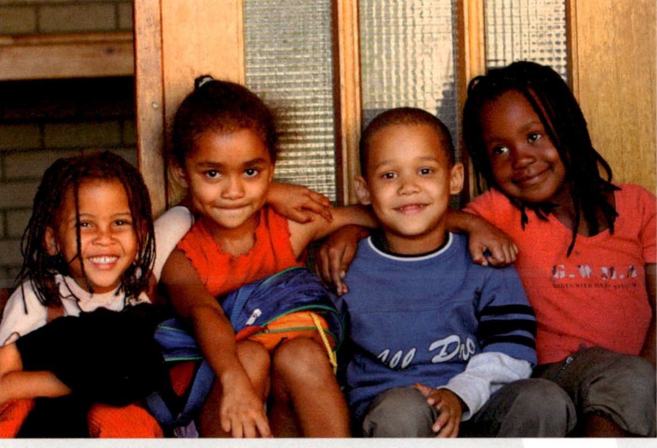

SOS Children's Villages Jamaica

SOS Children's Villages Jamaica operates the only long-term family-based care on the island. The late legendary country singer-songwriter, Johnny Cash, was one of SOS Jamaica's earliest supporters in 1974, when he and his wife June Carter helped fund the construction of the SOS Village in Barrett Town. SOS children are ensured the protection of a family, an education and life skills training with the aim of becoming responsible citizens in society:

- Over 200 children live in two SOS Children's Villages: Stony Hill and Barrett Town
- 36 teens reside in four SOS Youth Facilities
- Two SOS Kindergartens and one SOS Primary School educate nearly 300 students

Vulnerable children outside the SOS villages in Jamaica are also benefiting from SOS programs. However, more funding is needed to expand the capacity of schools to accommodate more community children.

Despite the many challenges in Jamaica that poverty creates, SOS education programs are succeeding. For instance, two high school girls who live at the SOS Youth Facility in Barrett Town are planning to attend university to study law and medicine!

For families in Jamaica, every day is a new struggle for the most basic necessities. Because children cannot be adequately cared for, parents often abandon them to an inadequate and overburdened social welfare system. SOS works to hold these families together with your support.

Invest in SOS and you invest in the life of a child in need.

For more information on SOS Children's Villages, please visit: www.sos-usa.org or call toll-free 1-888-SOS-4KIDS.

SOS Children's Villages - USA • 1200 G Street NW, Suite 550 • Washington, DC 20005 • www.sos-usa.org

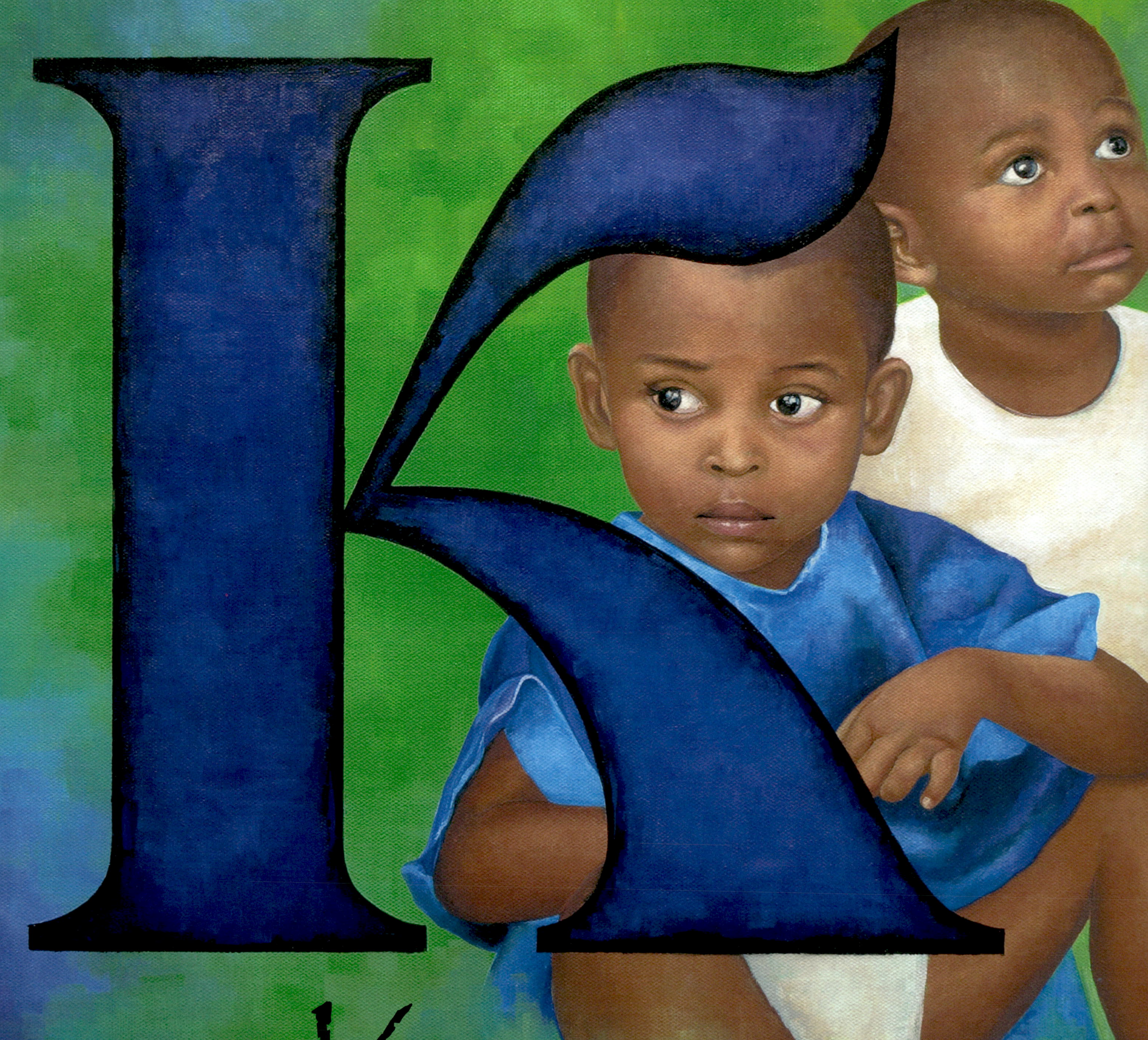

K is for Kenya

Waiting

We are really hungry.
Our stomachs hurt so bad.
Our mother, she is very sick
Same sickness took our dad.

As we sit here all alone
Waiting for her to die,
I wonder who will feed us.
Try my hardest not to cry.

All I feel is emptiness,
My tummy and my chest.
I see my mama close her eyes.
We wait and watch her rest.

Her eyes they never open.
It's getting dark outside.
The emptiness turns to fear.
I think our mother died.

"Children seldom have a proper sense of their own tragedy, discounting and keeping hidden the true horrors of their short lives, humbly imagining real calamity to be some prestigious drama of the grown-up world."

–Shirley Hazzard, Australian born American Author

About "Waiting"

"MY SISTER is six years old. There are no adults living with us. I need clothes and shoes. And water also, inside the house. But especially, somebody to tuck me and my sister in at night." Apiwe, age thirteen, is among a staggering number of AIDS orphans trying to cope with both life and death in Kenya.

It is estimated that by 2010, one-third of Africa's children will be orphaned because of AIDS. Kenya is among the African countries hardest hit by this pandemic. Hundreds of thousands of people have already died, leaving children behind, and at the mercy of a society that stigmatizes and often excludes them. In some cases, grandparents shoulder the burden, but life is dismal and often hopeless even with their best efforts. In many cases, the grandparents are too old or ill themselves, and extended families lack the financial resources to help. In the worst cases, children are left to fend for themselves. Neglected and unable to afford school fees, these children are at risk of exploitation by ruthless segments of Kenyan society. They are also more prone to engaging in activities and behaviors that will most certainly guarantee them a similar fate.

In recent years, some progress has been made in Kenya's daunting fight against AIDS. Yet, the current political climate within the country has the potential to unravel these efforts, wiping away the strides Kenya has made. As politics continue to pit neighbor against neighbor and tribe against tribe, children are left vulnerable and unprotected. Since the violence that erupted after the election results were announced on December 29th, 2007, Kenya has been on a slippery slope of insecurity, chaos and ethnic tension. An estimated nine hundred lives have been lost in violent outbreaks and as many as three hundred thousand people have been displaced. A once thriving economy has been brought to a near standstill.

While it might appear that the heat of Kenya's most recent political fires has died down, and the threat of genocide has been quieted to some degree, for people living in Kenya, the aftermath and simmering frustrations are far from benign. Food insecurity is on the rise because of the vast number of farmers forced to flee their lands and abandon their crops. Ethnic lines are still drawn and a heavy blanket of unease hangs over most of the country. The basic infrastructure that provides protection and services for citizens has been crippled, leaving the poor, displaced, sick and young, more exposed to both opportunistic and ethnically motivated crimes.

Considered an "emergency within an emergency," the war on AIDS and the future of Kenya's AIDS orphans lie at the center. Increased vulnerability, a significant rise in rape cases, lack of access to sustained medical care for people with the HIV virus, and impaired efforts of aid organizations threaten to worsen an already grave situation.

Over and over, around the globe, we see it: people fighting over political agendas, another tug-of-war of power, another clash of cultures, another futile battle to dominate land and resources that we must ultimately share. Kenya represents another place in the world where political unrest and the pursuit of power and control has become a tragic distraction from the things we should be doing to improve the world and the lives of the children inheriting it.

Did you know… Approximately two million of Kenya's estimated thirty million citizens are infected with the HIV virus?

blood:water mission

Blood:Water Mission is a non-profit organization founded by the members of the multi-platinum, Grammy Award-winning band, Jars of Clay, to address the HIV/AIDS crisis in Africa.

Our Mission:

To tangibly reduce the impact of the African HIV/AIDS pandemic, to promote clean blood and clean water in Africa, and to build equitable, sustainable and personal community links.

Our Vision:

To eradicate AIDS and the injustice that perpetuates it through personal and communal transformation.

"Clean water is a powerful way to begin a large scale conversation about AIDS. The 1000 Wells Project is a simple campaign that has very little controversy surrounding it. It is difficult to argue whether or not a person should have clean water. It is also difficult to deny the equation: $1= clean water for 1 person for 1 year. And it is vital that the church begin to build relationships with African communities. When a well is built, a conversation is started, a relationship between the church and the community benefiting from the project begins. This is the seed of a worldview shift. This is what excites us about this project."

-Dan Haseltine of Jars of Clay

- **Did you know that millions of Africans lack access to clean water?**
- **Did you know that people living with HIV/AIDS are dependent on clean water to survive?**
- **Did you know that $1 provides one year of clean water for an African?**

We recognize that numbers and statistics are hard to grasp, and that sometimes a step back is necessary to conceptualize the enormity of the HIV/AIDS crisis. Yet we also know that simply standing from a distance with arms thrown in the air is not a solution. We believe in pressing inward, in building relationships and bridges with communities in Africa. We believe in hearing personal stories and walking alongside brothers and sisters who have demonstrated strength and faith in the midst of desperate and tragic situations.

We hold fast to the conviction that we are all responsible for being good stewards of our time, our resources and our compassion in a broken world.

Every person has something to give in return for what has been received.

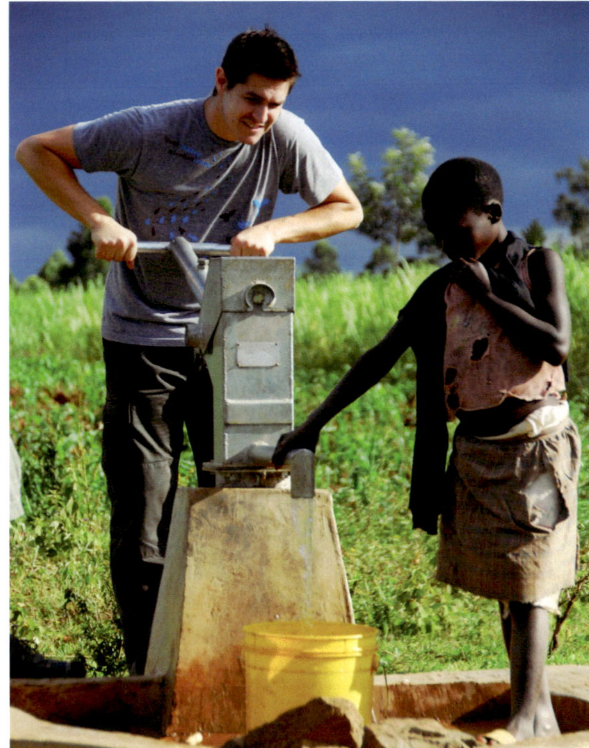

This, then, is the Blood:Water Mission, committed to clean blood and clean water to fight the HIV/AIDS pandemic, to build clean wells in Africa, to support medical facilities caring for the sick, to make a lasting impact in the fight against poverty, injustice and oppression in Africa through the linking of needs, talents and continents, of people and resources.

"As a fan, I don't think anyone has had a bigger voice than the activists in Jars of Clay."

–Bono of U2

We need you and they need you. Please join us on this journey of hope and care.

Blood:Water Mission • PO Box 60381 • Nashville, TN 37206 • www.bloodwatermission.com

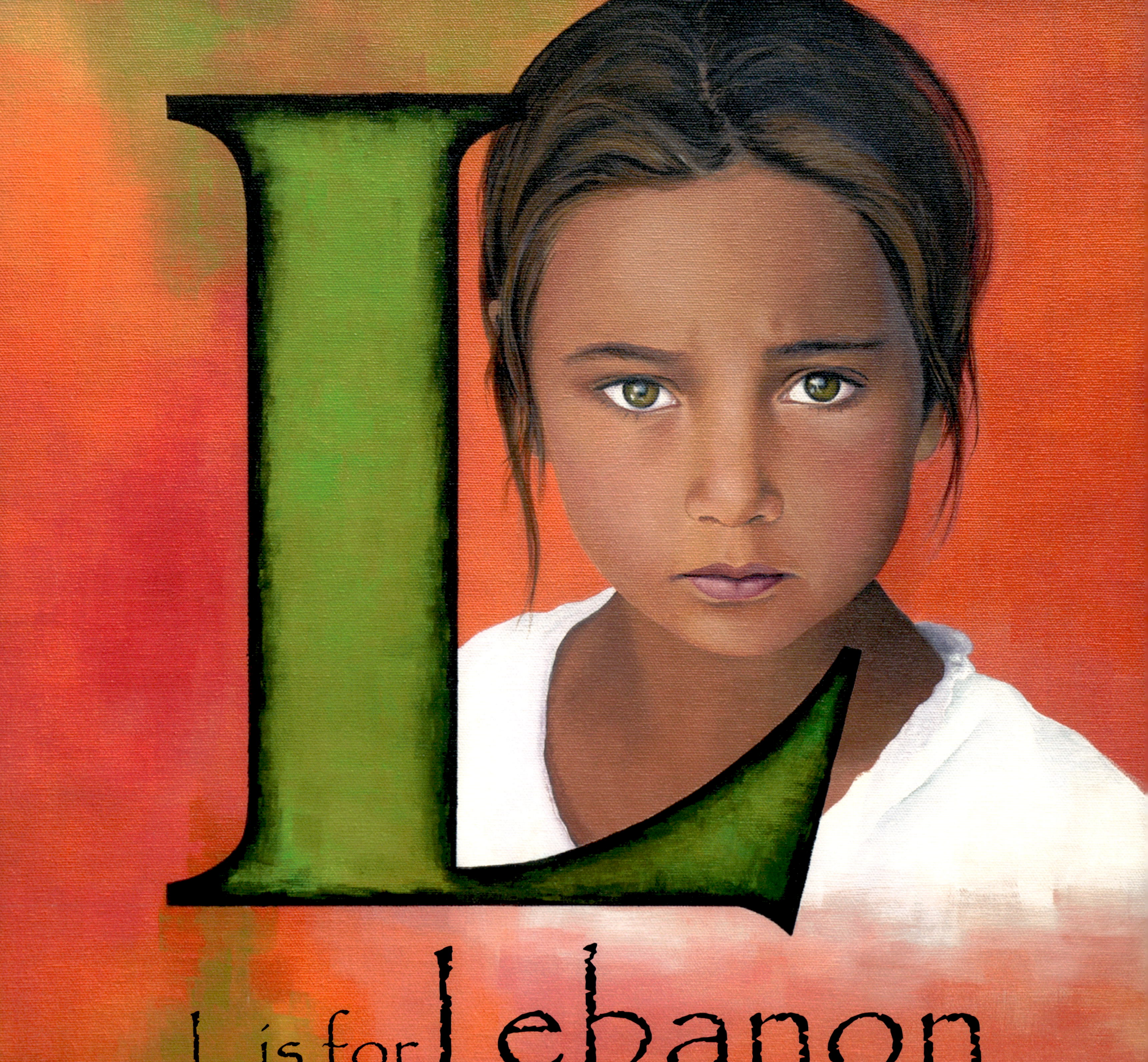
L is for Lebanon

My Eyes

My country has been at war
For years and years I'm told.
I don't exactly know how many,
But more than I am old.

My brother has learned to hate
And now he wants to fight.
My mother is afraid we'll die
From a bomb dropped in the night.

I don't know what to think.
My eyes have seen too much.
I feel the danger everywhere.
It's close enough to touch.

What was that?
It hurts so bad.
How come I can't see?
I hear them crying.
Is that my dad?
Are they crying over me?

"Convince an enemy, convince him that he's wrong. To win a bloodless battle, the victory is long. A simple act of faith, reason over might. To blow up his children would only prove him right."

–Gordon Sumner

About "My Eyes"

WALKING through a toy store, one cannot help but notice aisle after aisle of war-related games and toys, some aimed at very young children. It is difficult to comprehend how anyone can correlate war with fun and games, but judging from the vast selection, indeed we do. Why are we teaching our children that violence is entertaining? In doing so, aren't we making it easier for young minds to disconnect from reality in a manner that leaves little room for compassion? War is not a game. In war, lives are destroyed, people die and the human suffering is beyond imagination.

When asked if he sleeps at night, an eight-year-old Lebanese boy replies, "A little. I panic and wake up because of the bombs coming down and exploding like this," and he makes the sound of an explosion and waves his hands in the air. In Lebanon and much of the Middle East, war is a real and heartbreaking fact of life. Lebanon is a place where children view the world through eyes filled with horror, not wonder. Instead of playing in a yard with a sandbox or play set, these children stand among debris and rubble, and occasionally the corpses of their loved ones. Imagine a child's struggle to reconcile what his eyes are telling him before his young mind can begin to understand what he is seeing.

Lebanon is a country that has for decades been torn apart by one conflict after another. It is a country where diverse secular and religious factions struggle for power and effective governing… and co-existence is an elusive concept. In the perpetual aftermath, there is destruction, loss of life, insecurity, economic instability, and deep emotional scars for the survivors. Incredibly disturbing is the frequency of civilian targets in recent conflicts, including the Second Lebanon War in 2006, between the Hezbollah paramilitary forces of Lebanon and the Israeli Army. During this thirty-three day eruption of violence, one-third of the casualties were children under the age of thirteen. Left behind from this recent war are land mines and unexploded Israeli cluster bombs that have killed numerous people and wounded hundreds more. Many of these victims are children. "I can still hear the explosions here," another Lebanese child says as she points to her head. "I have nightmares." In Lebanon today, new conflicts continue to arise, leaving those living in refugee camps and other innocent people hopeless and vulnerable to more violence and instability.

Children should never be pawns of this violence, or at the mercy of a political agenda that furthers the pursuits of unscrupulous people and military regimes. Children are not responsible for their government's poor choices, and they should not be punished by their government's political and cultural enemies. The image of a child writing a message on a missile before it is launched is unnerving evidence of what children are learning in these climates of violence. The image of a little boy whose body has been mangled by an explosion is gut-wrenching evidence of a message received and innocence shattered.

We live in a world desensitized by the "pretend world of violence," due in part to the fact that we allow our children to enact war games and play with violent toys. Perhaps we need to be reminded that war is a brutal, ugly display of human shortcomings, where death is final with no reset, no second chance…game over.

Did you know… Due to the prevalence of civilian targets in the Second Lebanon War, over one-third of the casualties were children?

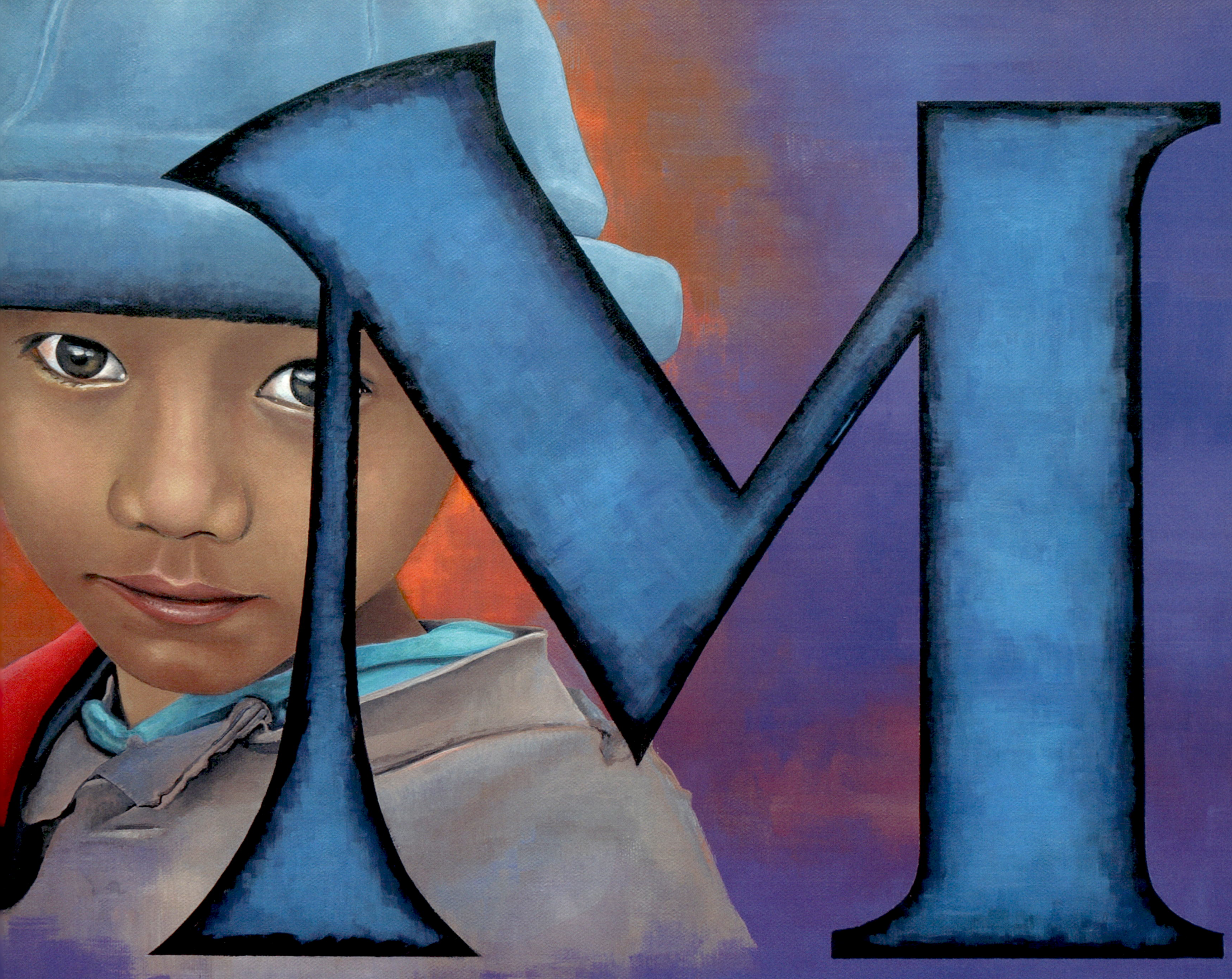

M is for Myanmar

The Price of Freedom

Today we had to leave our home.
My dad said it was best.
We've been walking through the forest.
I wish that we could rest.

My dad says we must hurry!
My sister won't stop crying.
My mom tells me to be brave.
I tell her that I'm trying.

I'm scared to death. I want to cry.
Please help me understand.
A flash of light! My sister screams!
I grab my mother's hand!

We forgot about the land mines
In our efforts to be free.
When we left today, we were four.
Now we're only three.

"The world is a dangerous place, not because of those who do evil, but because of those who look on and do nothing."

–Albert Einstein, Physicist

About "The Price of Freedom"

THROUGHOUT THE WORLD, individuals are held up on pedestals, celebrated and adored for different reasons, some more noble than others. It is the world's icons of peace who stand taller in their humility and simple conviction than any others. Aung San Suu Kyi is one such icon. A Nobel Peace Prize winner and democracy activist, she has been under house arrest in Burma (also referred to as Myanmar) for twelve of the past eighteen years. Although her courageous efforts have not yet produced the freedom she so fervently wants for the people of Burma, her convictions remain unshaken.

Aung San Suu Kyi, "is a woman who is taking on a brutal military dictatorship with nothing more than the truth in her heart and the support of her people," says Jack Healey, founder of the Human Rights Action Center. Although she was elected as prime minister with an eighty-two percent majority in 1990, instead of recognizing her victory, the military rulers of Burma locked her up along with many other members of her party.

While under military rule for more than forty-five years, Myanmar has gone from a resource rich and economically promising nation to one of the world's poorest countries. Human rights abuses are rampant. The military attacks and burns down villages, using civilians not only as forced labor, but also as human "minesweepers." The authorities steal food from families and prevent them from harvesting their own crops. These atrocities go unchecked, forcing thousands to flee their homes in search of food and safety. Since 1996, thousands of villages have been destroyed, more than six hundred thousand people have been displaced internally, and more than a million and a half have been forced to flee to other countries. The military operates in a state of impunity, as if it is their right to use civilians as expendable pawns. The Myanmar government is the only government in the world that used antipersonnel mines on a regular basis throughout 2006. These silent, indiscriminate weapons present a daily challenge for hundreds of thousands of civilians living in conflict zones.

Because of the government's increasing unpopularity with the people of Burma, the military forces are commonly replenished by forcing children as young as ten years old into their ranks. Burmese children are often treated like commodities, bought and sold by army recruiters…a practice kept neatly hidden, not only from most of the world but also from the country's own citizens. There are no firm numbers as to how many child soldiers currently fill the ranks of Myanmar's different armies, but evidence indicates that there are thousands.

With so many violations occurring blatantly and without consequences from the international community, what will become of Burma under these conditions? Gentle diplomacy doesn't seem to work when a government holds itself above the law. According to David Scott Mathison of Human Rights Watch, "Only consistent pressure from the rest of the world, and in particular Burma's neighbors and chief allies, will result in change for Burma's beleaguered people."

"Please use your liberty to promote ours." In these seven words, Aung San Suu Kyi sums up the very concept of human rights activism. The concept is unflawed, only apathy and indifference stand between the world and freedom.

Did you know… In Myanmar, the military reportedly attacks civilians, burns villages, and uses people as slave labor, forcing thousands to flee for safety and freedom?

U.S. CAMPAIGN FOR BURMA

Mobilizing a Global Effort for Human Rights, Democracy, and an End to Mass Atrocities

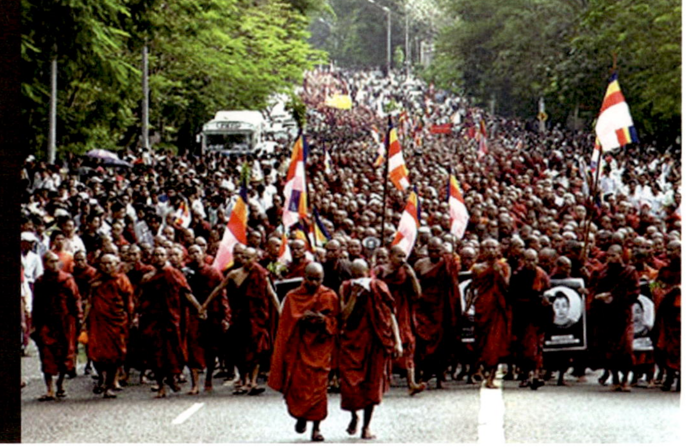

The Campaign

The United States Campaign for Burma is a U.S.-based membership organization dedicated to empowering grassroots activists around the world to bring about an end to the military dictatorship in Burma. Through public education, leadership development initiatives, conferences, and advocacy campaigns at local, national and international levels, USCB works to empower Americans and Burmese dissidents-in-exile to promote freedom, democracy, and human rights in Burma and raise awareness about the egregious human rights violations committed by Burma's military regime.

The leadership of USCB is comprised of seasoned human rights advocates, with experience both inside and outside the U.S. government. The board and staff, which include former Congressional staff, former Burmese political prisoners, and experienced advocates, are dedicated to increasing the profile of Burma and seeking solutions to the country's decades-long conflict.

The Crisis in Burma

Burma is one of the most forgotten crises in the world. The military has ruled the country for decades and the government tries with all its ruthless power to keep its people from speaking out to the world about what is happening there. They have locked up the democracy leader, Aung San Suu Kyi for 12 of the past 17 years. She is the world's only imprisoned Nobel Peace Prize winner, her teachings of peace and non-violence have inspired millions around the world. Even though her party, the National League for Democracy (NLD) won a landslide victory in the 1990 elections they were never allowed to take office.

The military junta has also maintained a fierce campaign against ethnic minority civilians. In the past ten years over 3,200 villages have been destroyed in eastern Burma. Millions have been forced from their homes. Rape is used as a weapon of war. There are more child soldiers than any other country in the world. Forced labor and land mines are also common tools the military uses.

The Saffron Revolution in 2007 showed an additional level of the harshness. Civilians and monks rose up to demand peace and stability in the country. Marching through the streets they spoke words of kindness only to be shot, beaten and imprisoned. During this intense time U.S. Campaign for Burma worked to rally public and political support for the monks and people of Burma.

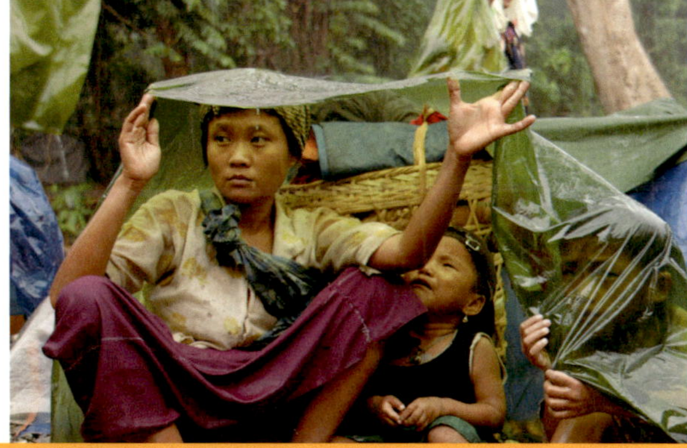

Join the battle to free Burma and end the suffering!

Nobel Peace Prize winner and Democratic leader, Aung San Suu Kyi is still imprisoned. Call for her release!

U.S. Campaign for Burma • 1444 N Street NW, Suite A2 • Washington, DC 20005 • 202-234-8022 • www.uscampaignforburma.org

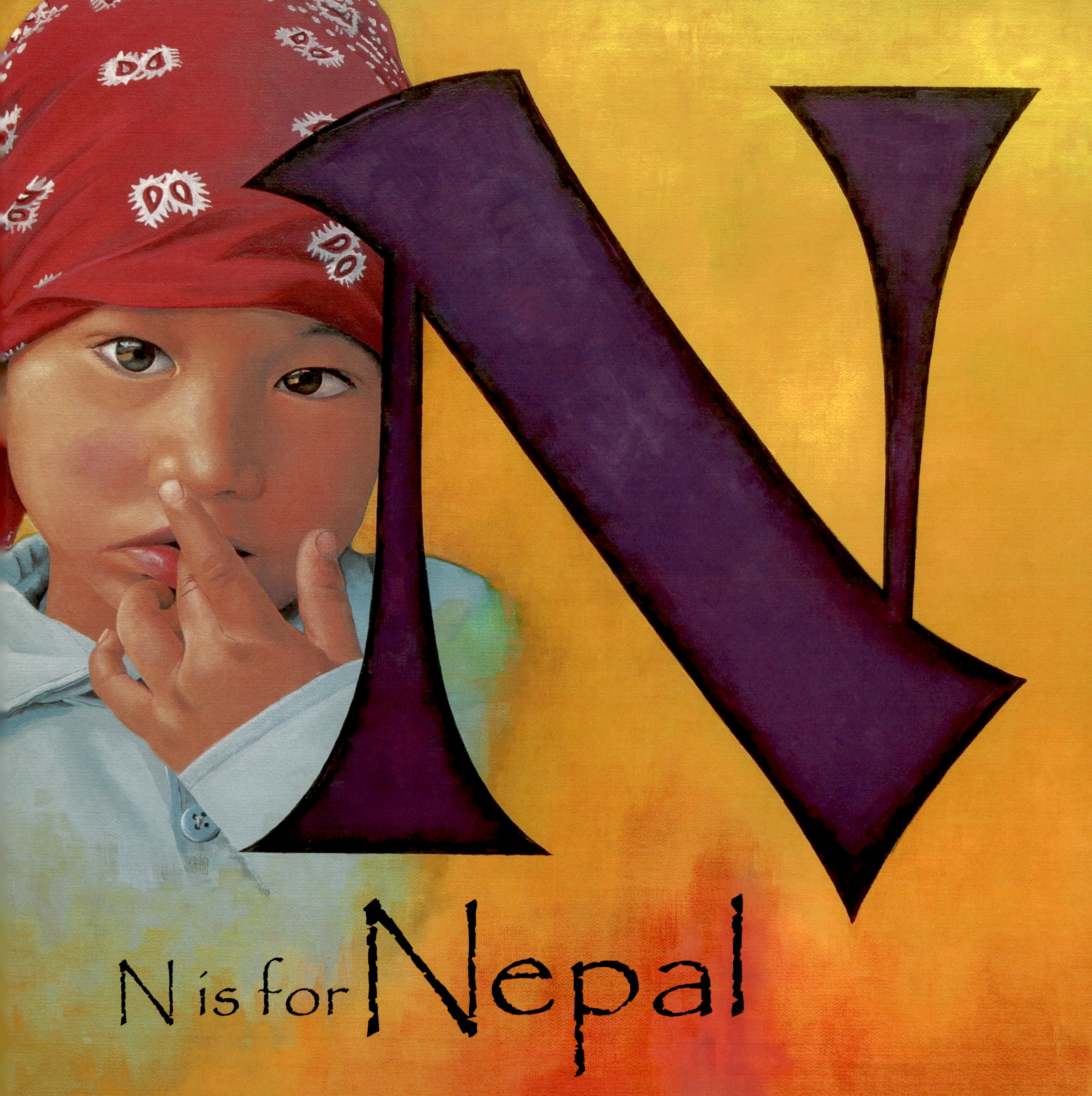
N is for Nepal

A Letter Never Sent

Little sister do you understand
Why they made me leave?
Has daddy ever told you?
Does mama ever grieve?

I guess it's what they had to do
Or so it's what they thought.
How much is a child worth?
Did they tell you what they got?

I have so many questions.
But it hurts to wonder why.
So ashamed and helpless.
Too numb to even cry.

I don't want to do the things
That they make me do.
I don't want to feel the way
I feel when they are through.

I wish that I could tell you
That things will be okay,
That I'll be coming home to you,
I know it's what you pray.

I love you baby sister,
But I have to say goodbye.
Please forgive me. It's not my fault.
I'm lost and want to die.

"I am not sure how many "sins" I would recognize in the world. Some would surely be defused by changed circumstances. But I can imagine none that is more irredeemably sinful than the betrayal, the exploitation, of the young by those who should care for them."

–Elizabeth Janeway, American Author and Critic

About "A Letter Never Sent"

"THE FIRST NIGHT they forced me to have sex. When I refused, they held me down, beat me and raped me. I was seven years old." Rescued at age ten, Gina, a soft-spoken Nepalese child, was dying from AIDS when she was immortalized in the PBS documentary *The Day My God Died*. This is one child's story, one child out of millions who have been and continue to be exploited. Considered one of the busiest places for trafficking today, thousands of young women and girls are trafficked from Nepal to India each year to become part of the sex trade. Some are lured by phony job offers which hold the promise of a better life. Many are abducted, while others are callously sold by members of their own families. However they get there, they share the same horrific experiences. They are kept against their will and forced to have sex with as many as twenty-five men in a single day. They are beaten, starved and burned with cigarettes when they don't comply. I think this bears repeating: these are girls as young as seven being forced to have sex with as many as twenty-five men in a single day. Let it sink in. It is critically important that we begin to understand the sheer magnitude of this issue.

The entire topic—the concept, the facts, the victims—breeds discomfort and the conscience begs us to turn away. We can't. We need to know the truth. Approximately eight hundred thousand people are trafficked across the globe every year. Eighty percent of these individuals are women and girls. Whether they are trafficked for the sex industry, forced labor or armed conflict, each one represents a modern-day slave, a person completely stripped of their human rights. Think in terms of the children and consider their ages. What must they be feeling? Fear? Pain? The images are brutally vivid…yet unimaginable.

In Nepal, there are two distinct types of "modern slavery" occurring at alarming rates. One is the trafficking of girls for the sex trade. The other is the culturally accepted practice of selling one's daughters into indentured servitude. The latter are referred to as Kamlaris. The girls are sold as young as six years of age to households far from home. They have no rights; they receive no money; and although an education is almost always promised, ninety percent never get to attend school. This practice is especially prevalent in poor, rural areas where it is considered a justifiable option to addressing poverty. The issue of sex trafficking is a thriving business, feeding off of greed, vulnerability and pure evil. In both cases, lives are destroyed, souls are consumed and innocence shattered.

When an issue moves beyond the status of a mere injustice and becomes one of the most profitable businesses on the planet, the challenges grow proportionately. Many experts question whether it is possible to stop human trafficking. Are too many people involved and benefitting from it? It is easy to become overwhelmed when an issue is pervasive. Turning a blind eye becomes an easy option as complacency settles back in and shock fades. We can't afford to be complacent. These children cannot be forgotten. While human trafficking may never go away, there is great potential to save lives through stricter laws, closer monitoring and stiffer punishments. In the case of cultural and poverty-driven indentured servitude, support, education and implementation of sustainable economic assistance is critical. Innocence should not be exportable. No one should sell it, no one should buy it and, most importantly, no one should have it stolen from them.

Did you know… The trafficking of girls from Nepal into India for the purpose of prostitution is one the busiest "slave traffic" of its kind anywhere in the world?

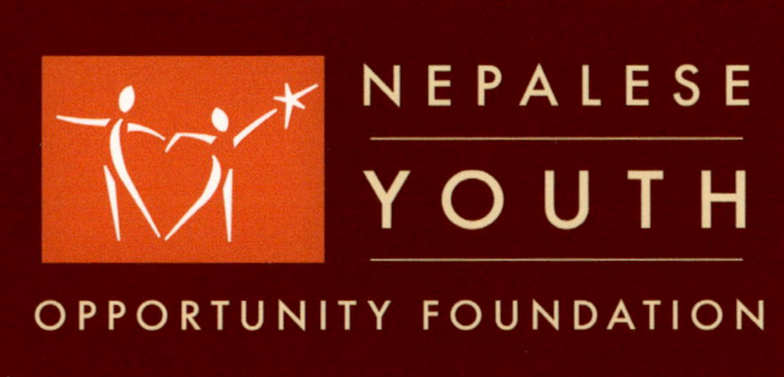

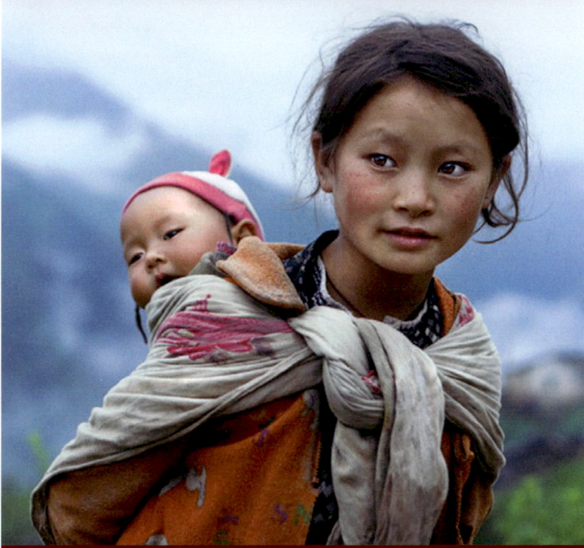

Our Mission

Established in 1990, the Nepalese Youth Opportunity Foundation (NYOF) is a U.S. based, non-profit organization devoted to bringing hope to the most destitute children in the beautiful but impoverished country of Nepal. With a personal touch, NYOF provides them with what should be every child's birthright – education, housing, medical care and loving support. Empowered to reach their potentials, these children blossom, enriching the world we all share.

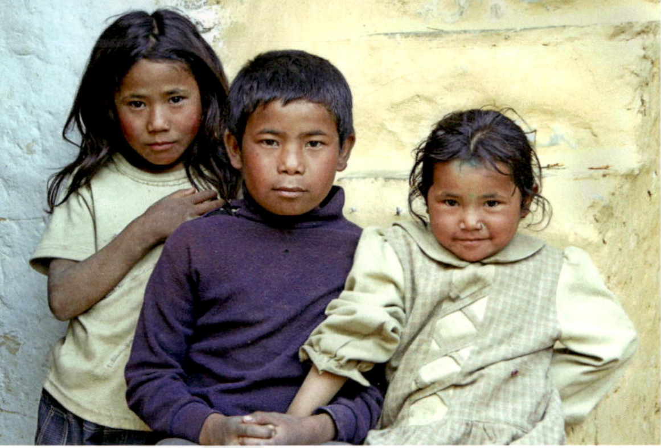

How We Work

NYOF leverages the wealth of developed countries to help Nepalese children. Because dollars go far in Nepal, we can literally change lives for pennies a day. It costs $75 a year to send a village child to school. $100 rescues a little girl from bonded labor and pays her school costs, and $250 restores a starving baby to health and educates the mother so the problem doesn't recur. The opportunity to help is irresistible.

Our partners in this work are private foundations and individuals around the world and non-governmental organizations in Nepal. NYOF's good governance has been recognized by Charity Navigator, America's largest independent evaluator of charities, which has granted NYOF a four-star rating, the highest possible, for effective and efficient administration of all donated funds.

- **Nutritional Rehabilitation Homes** - Welcome to the home of miracles. Imagine a child seriously malnourished – unresponsive and pitifully frail. Jump to six weeks later; imagine a bouncing, happy child with a parent now educated in child nutrition and care. We see these miracles every day. NYOF funds and manages six residential rehabilitation centers for severely malnourished children in Kathmandu and in rural areas of Nepal. The children and their mothers come to live at these centers, where we restore the child's health while educating the mother in child care, including preparation of nutritious meals, using foods readily available in rural Nepal. Our field workers later follow up in the villages.

Malnutrition is the leading cause of death of Nepali children under age five. NYOF's goal is to build 14 Nutritional Rehabilitation Homes, one in each of the zonal communities.

- **Liberating Girls From Indentured Servitude** - In parts of western Nepal, many indigenous families subsist as farm laborers. Unable to make ends meet, thousands of them have been forced into a desperate trade – selling their daughters to work in faraway cities as bonded servants. Some of these little girls are as young as six! They slave from dawn to late at night in private homes or as dishwashers in tea houses. The fathers receive an average of $50 a year for their daughters' services, and the girls get nothing. The families don't want to sell their daughters, but they can't do without the income. The situation is tailor-made for abuse. Working closely with local communities, NYOF helps parents bring their daughters home from the city and provide a tiny piglet or goat – much valued in this culture – which the families can raise on food scraps, and sell for the same amount their daughters would have earned. We then pay all expenses for the girls to attend the local school.
- **J & K House** - NYOF operates two homes for 60 children: J House (for boys) and K house (for girls). These children are the most vulnerable among those we help. They were orphans, living on the streets, or were abandoned by their parents. Others are disabled. We shower them with attention and provide loving support, education, and medical expenses. We commit for the long term (through college) and give them what is usually the first real sense of security in their lives. Many of the children are sponsored by donors, who often become quite close to the child, even from afar.
- **Scholarships** - NYOF intervenes at critical points to make education possible for children who have no other hope. We support over 4,000 youngsters from kindergarten through medical school. Our students attend private and government schools in busy Kathmandu and in rural villages that are often more than a day's walk from any road. We also help train teachers and build and improve schools.

Nepalese Youth Opportunity Foundation • 3030 Bridgeway, Suite 123 • Sausalito, CA 94965 • 415-331-8585 • www.nyof.org

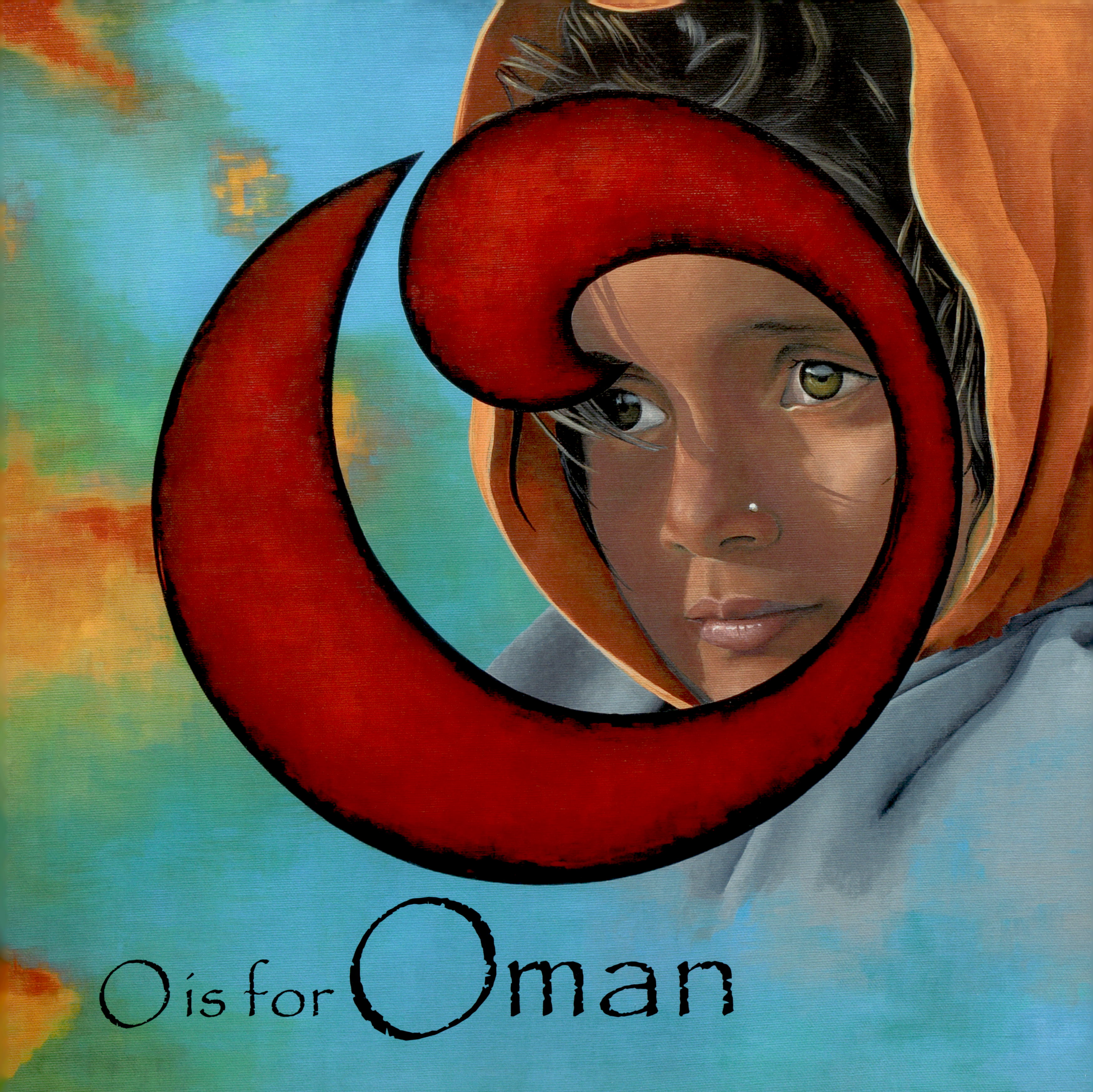
O is for Oman

Who Makes Your Clothes?

What's it like to be a child?
I don't even know.
I work in a factory.
All I do is sew.

I work at least twelve hours,
Sometimes even more,
In a place that's small and dingy,
After sleeping on the floor.

A place that isn't clean or safe,
Where children sometimes die.
A place where children live in fear,
Too afraid to cry.

Children make good workers.
We are vulnerable and small.
They can pay us very little,
Sometimes not at all.

With no one to protect us
From the beatings and the rape,
The sweatshop is our life.
A life we can't escape.

"180 million kids are engaged in the worst forms of child labour. Put it all together and it is not only morally unacceptable, but politically dangerous."

–Juan Somavia, Director-General, International Labour Office

About "Who Makes Your Clothes?"

OMAN is a relatively small country governed by Sultan Qaboos bin Said al-Said. It is considered an absolute monarchy, and its citizens can express their views only in a very limited way. Non-citizens, who make up eighty-five percent of the private-sector workforce, have little or no rights, and expressing their views in regard to labor abuses is apt to get them imprisoned or deported. The U.S. State Department has reported Oman for human trafficking and forced labor abuses, and the country is currently considered a Tier 3 in their Trafficking in Persons Report. Countries with a Tier 3 status are given a failing grade based on violations as well as lack of adequate effort to eliminate the problem or prosecute the offenders.

In January of 2006, the U.S. and Oman signed a Free Trade Agreement (FTA). To understand the significance and potential impact of this agreement, consider a similar agreement that was signed between the U.S. and Jordan, another small country in the Middle East, in 2001. By 2006, according to the nonpartisan National Labor Committee, the number of sweatshops had increased and conditions for workers had worsened significantly since the FTA was signed. Additionally, under the FTA, there was a twenty-fold surge in the amount of goods produced from Jordanian sweatshops coming into the U.S. What is more difficult to quantify is the human suffering that went into these products. This comparison is critically important because this undercover investigation illuminates how the U.S.-Jordan agreement, a deal with stronger labor rights provisions than the Oman deal, resulted in a major expansion of sweatshops.

There is a widespread and terribly false perception that sweatshops, even with their pitifully low wages, help poor people eventually climb out of poverty. Sweatshop workers and child laborers are trapped, often forced against their will, into a cycle of exploitation and abuse. In the deplorable conditions uncovered in Jordan, workers were forced to work forty-eight hour shifts without sleep, subjected to violent physical and psychological abuse, forced to relinquish their passports, and ultimately denied their wages.

Sweatshops are a widespread and pervasive problem. Corporate greed, global competition and consumerism are all at the core of the issue. Corporations thrive on opportunities to do business in foreign markets. Taking advantage of weak laws and regulations that exploit human beings creates a successful recipe for increasing corporate profits. It is estimated that the U.S.-Oman agreement will increase the U.S. import of apparel manufactured in Oman by sixty-six percent. Oman is a country that only fines its people thirteen hundred dollars for the worst forms of child labor, and a second offense in punishable by less than a month in jail. Thus the question must be raised…Who will make these clothes?

Every day U.S. citizens use products or dress in garments that were produced at great human cost without even realizing it. The old adage, "What you don't know won't hurt you," ought to be changed to "What you don't know might be killing someone else." It would be hard for most of us to envision just how bad these environments are; even harder to imagine is how young the victims sometimes are and how extensive the abuses they endure. Perhaps if we really understood, we would become more compassionate and less frenzied consumers. Even more importantly, we might actually raise our voices against trade agreements that make it convenient to turn children into slaves.

Did you know… In Oman, the fine for using children in the worst forms of child labor is only thirteen hundred dollars?

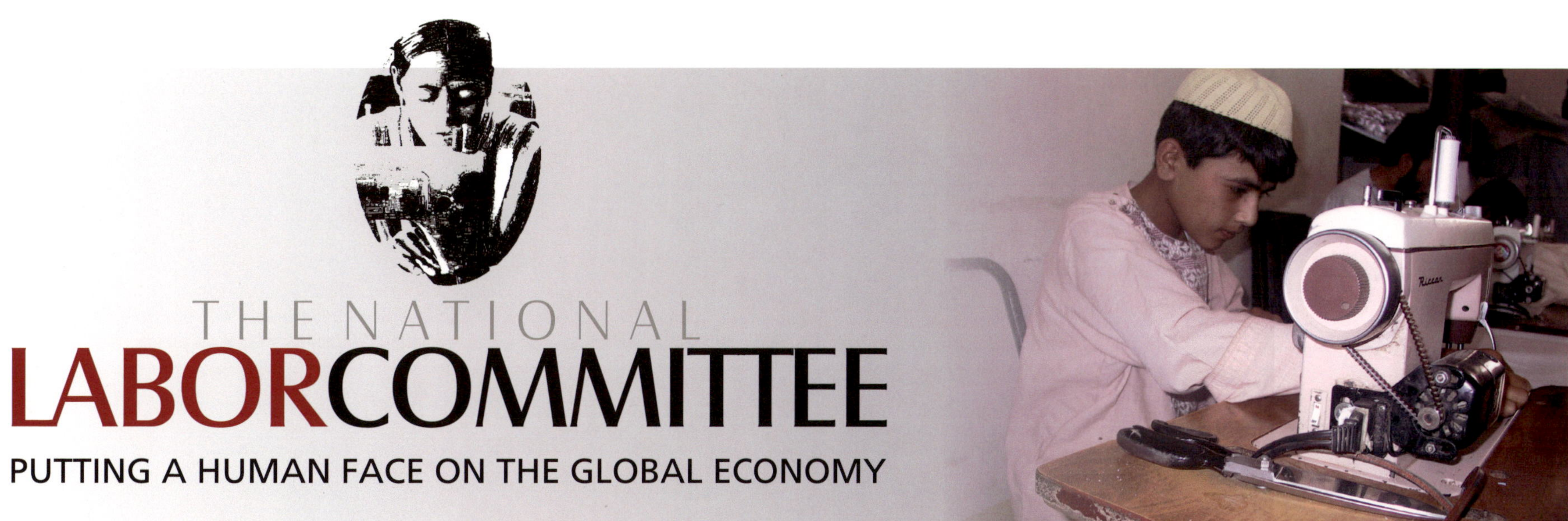

Mission Statement

Transnational corporations now roam the world to find the cheapest and most vulnerable workers. The people who stitch together our jeans and assemble our CD-players are mostly young women in Central America, Mexico, Bangladesh, China and other poor nations, many working 12 to 14-hour days for pennies an hour. The lack of accountability on the part of our U.S. corporations–now operating all over the world, and the resulting dehumanization of this new global workforce is emerging as the overwhelming moral crisis of the 21st century. The struggle for rule of law in the global economy–to ensure respect for the fundamental rights of the millions of workers producing goods for the U.S. market–has become the great new civil rights movement of our time.

The mission of the National Labor Committee is to help defend the human rights of workers in the global economy. The NLC investigates and exposes human and labor rights abuses committed by U.S. companies producing goods in the developing world. We undertake public education, research and popular campaigns that empower U.S. citizens to support the efforts of workers to learn and defend their rights. As they fight for the right to work in dignity, in healthy and safe workplaces and to earn a living wage, we will work with them to provide international visibility and backing for their efforts–and to press for international legal frameworks with effective enforcement mechanisms that will help create a space where fundamental internationally recognized worker rights can be assured.

Our Accomplishments

The NLC's work is helping to coalesce a new and diverse coalition that includes religious, labor, women's, student, civil rights, solidarity, policy and grassroots groups to catalyze popular campaigns based on our original research to promote worker rights and pressure companies to end human and labor abuses. With a database of over 22,000 organizations and individuals, we serve as an information center, distributing our literature and videos. In just the last few years the NLC has:

- Helped bring massive and widespread media coverage to worker and human rights issues, raising them to a national level of public debate;
- Established ground-breaking models for independent monitoring of factories by local human rights and religious groups;
- Successfully pressured dozens of companies - including the Gap, Kathie Lee Gifford/Wal-Mart, and the Walt Disney Company - to improve conditions in supplier plants and to respect human and worker rights.

The National Labor Committee views worker rights in the global economy as indivisible and inalienable human rights and we believe that now is the time to secure them for all on the planet.

Please Note:

The National Labor Committee does not currently do work in Oman, nor do we make any claims in regard to Oman and the existence of sweatshops.

"If the American retailers paid only 25 cents more per garment, the total in Bangladesh would be $898 million- more than eight times current U.S. aid"

National Labor Committee • 75 Varick St., Suite 1500 • New York, NY 10013 • www.nlcnet.org

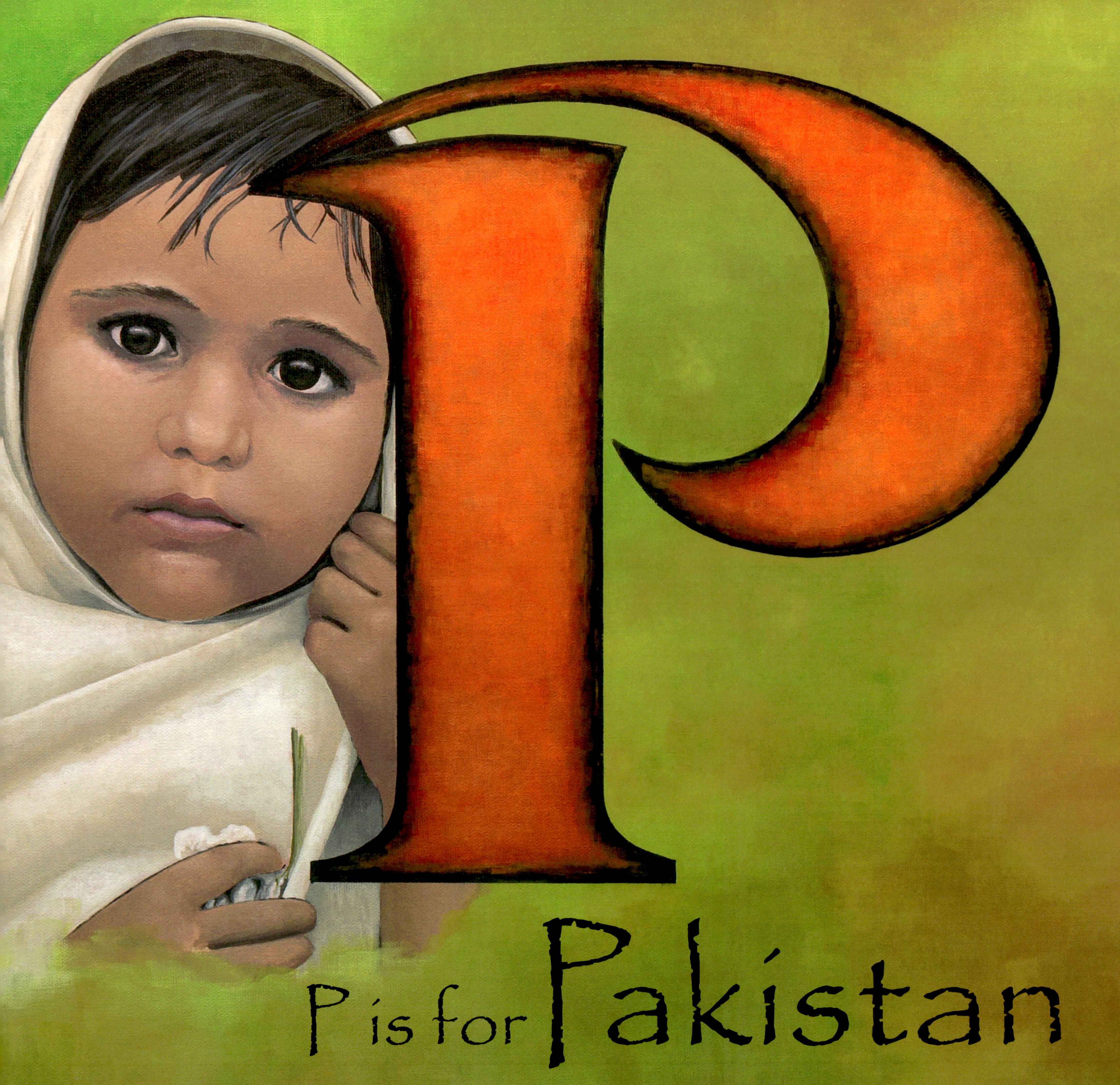
P is for Pakistan

Innocence Traded

Today they gave me to a man.
Someone tell me why.
Will he hurt me?
Don't they wonder?
Don't they see me cry?

They say my father was in trouble.
He had a debt to pay.
So it was me, I'm only four,
That he gave away.

I wish I were old enough
To understand this life.
To understand why a child,
Can be traded as a wife.

Please don't beat me.
I'll work harder.
I promise that I can.
Daddy, please take me back,
Don't leave me with this man!

"The connection between women's human rights, gender equality, socioeconomic development and peace is increasingly apparent."

–Mahnaz Afkhami, Women's Human Rights Activist

About "The Price of Innocence"

IN SOME PLACES in the world, children are traded like commodities, used to repay a debt or handed over as retribution for a crime committed by another member of their family. One such place is the Punjab province of Pakistan.

Because of tribal customs that continue in spite of government ban, young women and girls are being used as compensation for grievances against male relatives. The marriages that these young women are traded into almost always take place while they are minors, often infants. They are customarily handed over at puberty.

With men old enough to be their fathers, sometimes old enough to be their grandfathers, these contract marriages are just another form of modern slavery. The girls become family servants. They are forced to tend to the needs of others even before they are mature enough to look after themselves. Rarely are they treated as a member of the family, but are instead subjected to cruelty and humiliation as a reminder that they were nothing more than payment of a debt. Too often this is the sum of their lives.

Child abuse in any form is a horrific and intolerable crime. This kind of child abuse, the betrayal and abandonment, the indifference and willingness to trade a child into unimaginable suffering is beyond comprehension. Why then does it exist? It exists because this issue is embedded deeply within a culture that believes it is a way to avoid blood feuds between rival clans. It is tolerated because the gender discrimination in Pakistan and other places around the world, simply doesn't recognize the rights of the girl child. Living under this kind of inequality, girls can be violated, beaten, raped, forced into marriage and even sold; their freedom stolen, their lives ruined…no one held accountable.

Cultural customs, however deeply rooted, that deny a person's inherent rights, especially those of children, must be changed. We cannot allow these practices that grate against our hearts and conscience to continue, regardless of how far back these customs or traditions date. No child anywhere in the world should be subject to such abuses because they were born into a particular region, ethnicity, or culture. Children, like the rest of us, deserve the freedom to decide for themselves what portion of their birthright they accept and what portion they reject.

While seldom mature enough to understand their own human rights or why they are abused, children are always old enough to feel the magnitude of pain that the world allows them to suffer.

Did you know… In Pakistan, female rape victims are reportedly imprisoned indefinitely for adultery?

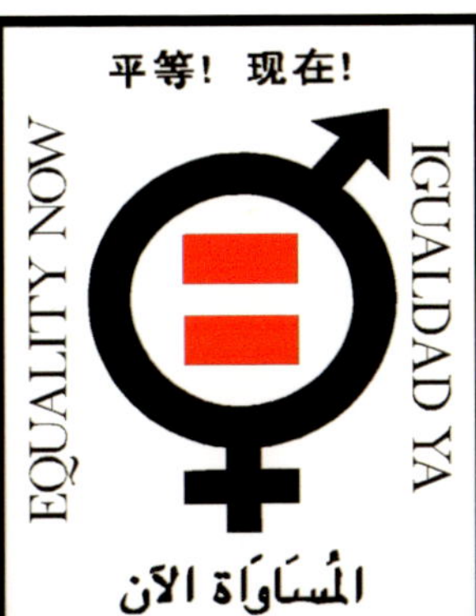

Equality Now

Ending Violence and Discrimination Against Women and Girls Around the World

Our Mission

Equality Now is an international human rights organization that works to protect and promote the civil, political, economic and social rights of women and girls. Issues of concern to Equality Now include: rape, trafficking, female genital mutilation (FGM), political participation, domestic violence, reproductive rights and gender discrimination. Equality Now's Women's Action Network is comprised of over 35,000 organizations and individuals in more than 160 countries.

The Power of the Individual

Individual voices play a critical role in ending violations against women. For over 15 years Equality Now has advanced the human rights of women and girls globally by channeling the collective outrage of individuals about women's rights abuses into strategic action. Holding governments accountable through public pressure via faxes, letters and phone calls by individual members has helped lead to important advances for women's rights, such as amending rape laws in Pakistan, stopping stoning in Iran, enforcing laws against FGM in Tanzania, shutting down sex tour operators in the US, and obtaining the right to vote in Kuwait.

Equality Now's work in Pakistan

In Pakistan, Equality Now has worked on justice for rape victims by campaigning for repeal of the Hudood Ordinances, advocating on behalf of Dr. Shazia, a rape survivor, and collaborating with Mukhtharan Mai, a women's rights advocate and gang-rape survivor.

Equality Now first highlighted one of Pakistan's laws, the Hudood Ordinances, in a campaign against discriminatory laws around the world in 2000. The Hudood Ordinances considered rape one of the offenses of zina and required either the confession of the perpetrator or the eye-witness testimony of at least four Muslim adult male witnesses to the rape. If she was unable to prove rape, a woman who reported rape to the police was vulnerable to prosecution herself under these Hudood Ordinances for fornication if she was unmarried or for adultery if she was married. Women who have been raped are still at risk of "honor" killings.

In 2005 Equality Now launched a Women's Action campaign specifically calling for repeal of the Hudood Ordinances on rape and highlighting the case of Dr. Shazia, a Pakistani physician who worked at a hospital run by Pakistan Petroleum Limited (PPL), a state-owned natural gas supplier in Pakistan and was attacked and raped in her home by an intruder. Dr. Shazia reported the crime to the police despite intense pressure from PPL doctors to keep silent. Instead of promoting the apprehension and punishment of her attacker, the government of Pakistan encouraged Dr. Shazia and her husband Khalid to flee the country, claiming it was unable to protect them from personal danger. Equality Now called on the Pakistani Government to repeal the discriminatory Hudood Ordinances and to ensure that Dr. Shazia's case is investigated and that those who are responsible for her rape are brought to justice.

In 2007 the Pakistan Senate Standing Committee on Petroleum and Natural Resources' examined PPL's response to the rape and assault as part of a larger investigation of the company, and reports suggest that the committee had recommended that PPL take steps to rectify its role in impeding justice for Dr. Shazia. Equality Now continues to demand that PPL be held accountable for its involvement in the obstruction of justice in Dr. Shazia's case.

In 2006, Pakistan's President Pervez Musharraf signed into law the Protection of Women (Criminal Laws) Amendment Act 2006. The Act, which was passed amid extensive debate and criticism from civil society and women's activists in Pakistan, amended the Hudood Ordinances, ostensibly in order to ensure better protection for women who were victims of rape, but it did not revoke the Hudood Ordinances in their entirety. Under the new law, judges have been given the authority to try rape cases exclusively under criminal law rather than Islamic law; the Act also includes safeguards to prevent charges of rape which do not result in convictions from being converted into charges of adultery and have removed the requirement of four male witnesses to provide evidence of rape. However the crime of 'fornication' has been inserted into the Pakistan Penal Code–charges for which are traditionally more likely to be brought against women than men.

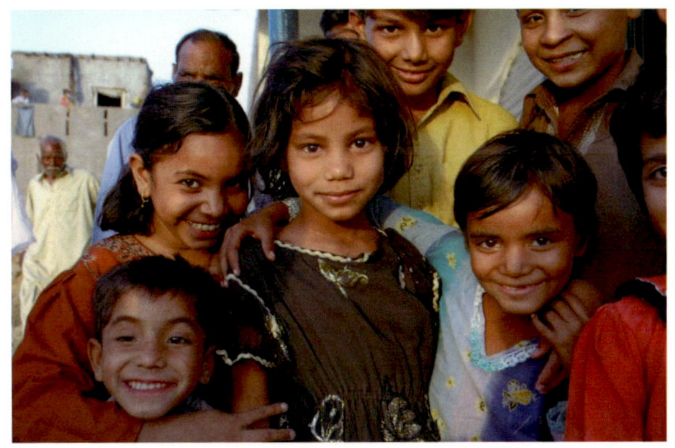

Equality Now

Equality Now • PO Box 20646 Columbus Circle Station • New York, NY 10023 USA • www.equalitynow.org

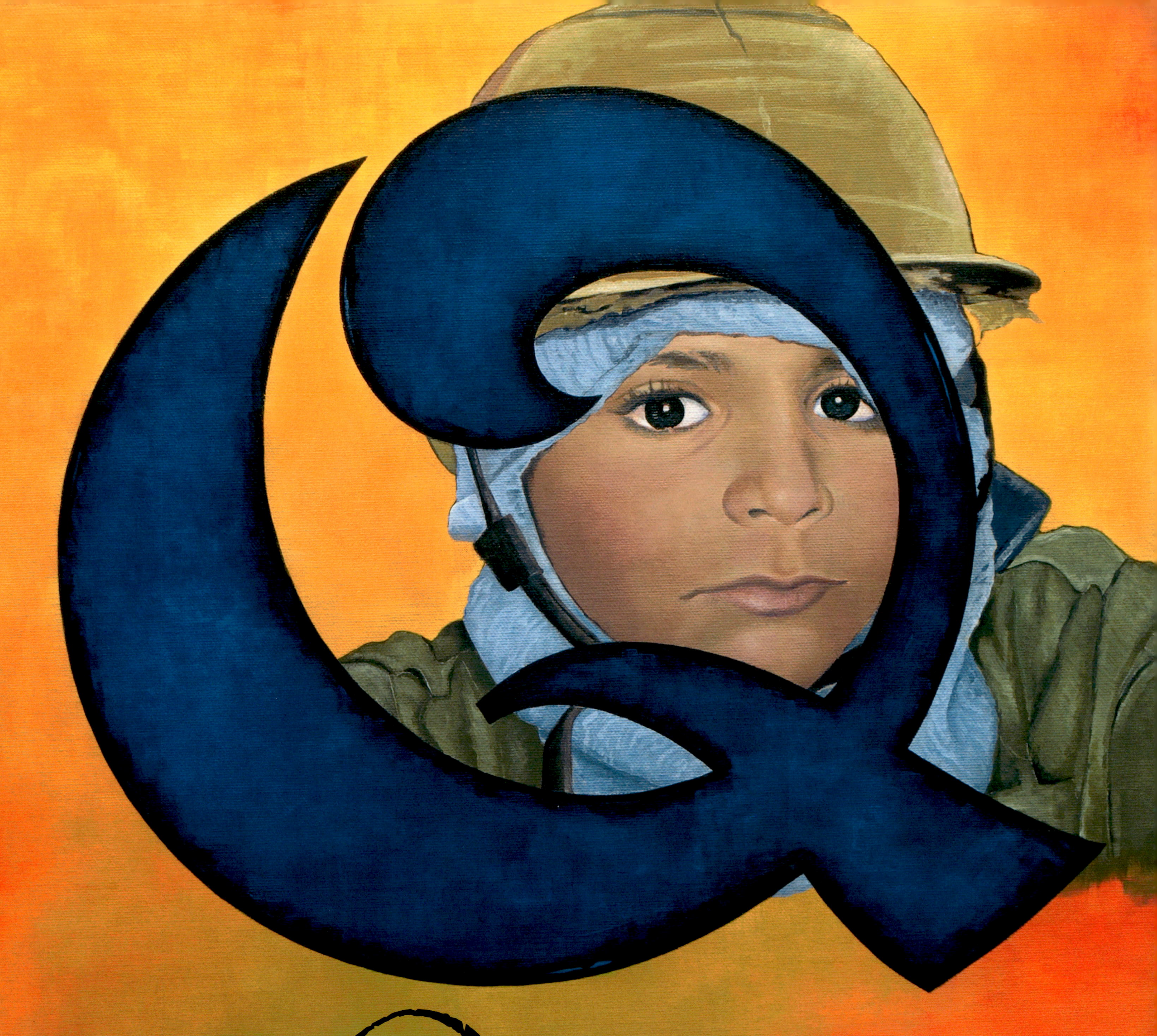

Q is for Qatar

Mama's Eyes

They took me from my home
And brought me to this place.
They strapped me to a camel's back
And taught me how to race.

I was just a little boy,
They like us very light.
And the camels, they run faster,
When we scream in fright.

I used to cry every night,
But it's been so many years.
Now I just have emptiness,
Where once there were my tears.

I try to remember what she looks like
And I wonder if she cries.
If I try really hard,
I can see my mama's eyes.

"So long as little children are allowed to suffer, there is no true love in the world."

–Isadora Duncan, American Dancer

About "Mama's Eyes"

WHEN WE THINK of human trafficking, a sickening and sobering concept, it usually conjures up images of young women trafficked for the sex trade. We rarely envision babies, boys as young as one, being abducted for the purpose of camel racing. It's almost inconceivable to imagine a child being taken from his mother's arms or sold by his own father only to be thrust into this dangerous and often deadly sport. Sadly, it's been happening for decades. Oil rich countries across the gulf are the destination of as many as forty thousand boys trafficked into the camel racing industry.

While in some places, it is part of a culture and the only source of income, camel jockeying is considered one of the worst forms of child labor in existence. Not only is it incredibly dangerous, the children used are underfed to maintain a minimal weight, physically and sexually abused, and made to work long and inhumane hours. They have little or no contact with their families and are subject to a life of absolute suffering and cruelty.

After much persistence and pressure from human rights groups, government bans on the use of children as camel jockeys were put into effect in 2005, in places like Kuwait, Qatar and UAE (United Arab Emirates). Since then, an effort has been made to locate the victims and reunite them with their families in their countries of origin. This has been a discouraging task for many reasons. In cases where children were sold by their parents, reunification is not always possible due to the high risk of the child being resold. Locating a child's family can be difficult when the children are abducted at such young ages that they don't even know where they are from. In cases where reunification is possible, the children are often mentally handicapped either from injury or stunted growth and almost never have normal communication or social skills. In these cases, the families, once located, often choose to hand the boys over to religious schools (Madrassas) that are funded by extremist groups in places like Pakistan. Rejected by society and their families, these children become pawns of groups who will likely mold them into the next generation of terrorists.

While the use of child camel jockeys has declined since the bans, there is video evidence recorded in 2007, that shows children still being used in Qatar, Oman, Kuwait and UAE. Additionally, there are still thousands of missing camel jockeys. According to reports, only about a thousand boys have been successfully returned to their homes. Boys that were supposed to be returned, have disappeared from the camel racing camps since the bans took effect. The speculation is that they are still being used as camel jockeys in unofficial camel races or have been smuggled across borders and into other territories. Wherever they are, they need to be found and every effort made to rehabilitate them. In so many cases the damage is irreparable, but the effort must still be made. It is critical that we condemn this practice as the evil it is, the perpetrators as the monsters they are and do whatever it takes to assure that not one more baby, not one more little boy, be made to suffer in this manner.

Did you know… An estimated forty thousand boys, many as young as two years in age, have been abducted into this dangerous and deadly sport?

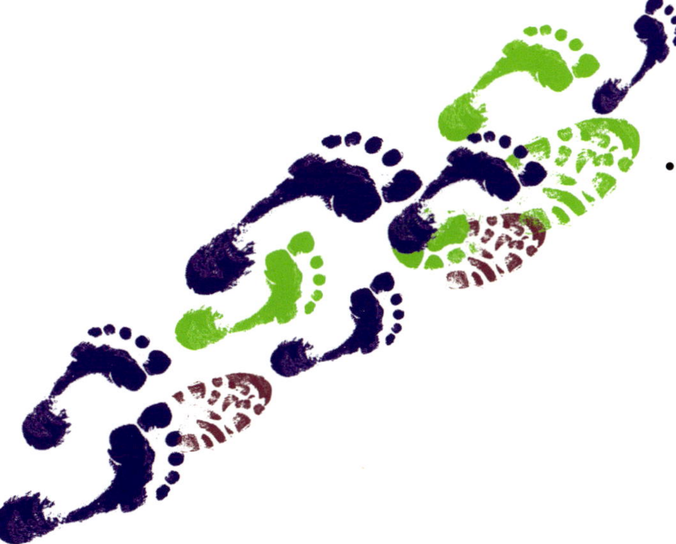

GLOBAL MARCH

Against Child Labour
Contra el Trabajo Infantil
Contre le Travail des Enfants

Our Mission

"The Global March Against Child Labour is a movement to mobilise worldwide efforts to protect and promote the rights of all children, especially the right to receive a free, meaningful education and to be free from economic exploitation and from performing any work that is likely to be harmful to the child's physical, mental, spiritual, moral or social development."

Global March Against Child Labour is a movement born out of hope and the need felt by thousands of people across the globe - the desire to set children free from servitude.

Our work focuses on the following:

- To build the campaigning, advocacy and lobbying capacity of our member organizations in the global south and in the transition countries, so that they can cooperate in playing their full role of watch dog in ensuring that exclusion in education is addressed as a matter of urgency and in the national consultations required by ILO Convention 182.
- To encourage policy coherence in ongoing efforts to combat social exclusion and poverty and to support decent work and education for all through better inter-ministerial and inter-agency coordination at the national, regional and global level, and particularly to ensure full implementation of ILO Conventions 182 and 138 and to achieve the Dakar goals.
- To launch an effective campaign against domestic child labor, addressing gender discrimination as the biggest obstacle to universal access to primary and secondary education, and supporting the campaign for a new ILO Convention to protect the rights of domestic workers.
- To continue to work for effective public policy to combat the causes, incidence and effects of trafficking of children nationally, regionally and globally
- To recognize and support the efforts of trade unions to strengthen their presence in those parts of the global economy in which child labor is prevalent in order to ensure that adults have decent work and that children are in school and not at work.

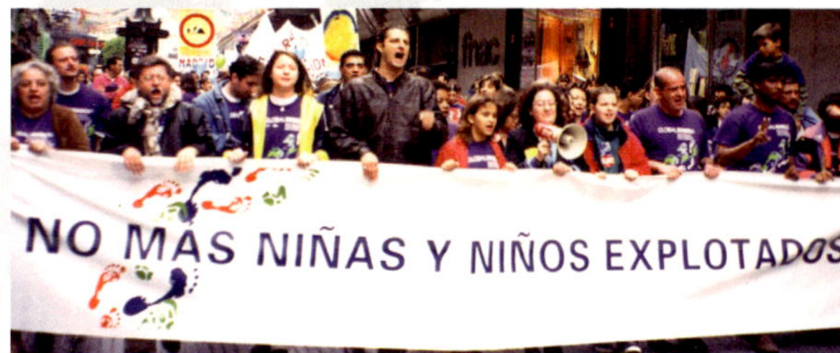

Our Achievements

Global March undertook 80,000 KM foot march across the globe to create awareness on children that are in worst forms of labor condition and contributed immensely in the ILO C 182 on worst forms of hazardous work. GM created the movement and spirit behind the formation of the Global Task Force on Child Labor and Education now anchored with the International Labor Organizations.

Our partner in India has organized raids to secure the release of close to 70 thousand children from forced labor and slavery.

They have busted the big names like GAP in their outsourcing supply chains and that has led to the company withdrawing products from some of their suppliers based in India.

GM is the force that has brought the issue of children that are being left out of the national plans on education for all as they are hardest to reach because they are working in the farms, factories and mines, identifying that the world has to do more to ensure that every child gets the opportunity in life to attend eight years of free full time quality education so that he can finish his/her basic education. The simple message being that the UN Commitment on Education for All cannot be realized if child labor is not stopped and elimination of child labor should be the ninth MDG.

Global March primarily works to eradicate child labor occurring in labor camps and sweatshops globally. For more information about the specific issue of camel jockeys and how to support the efforts to find and rehabilitate the victims please visit: www.ansarburney.org

Global March Against Child Labour • PO Box 4479 • Kalkaji, New Delhi 110019, India • www.globalmarch.org

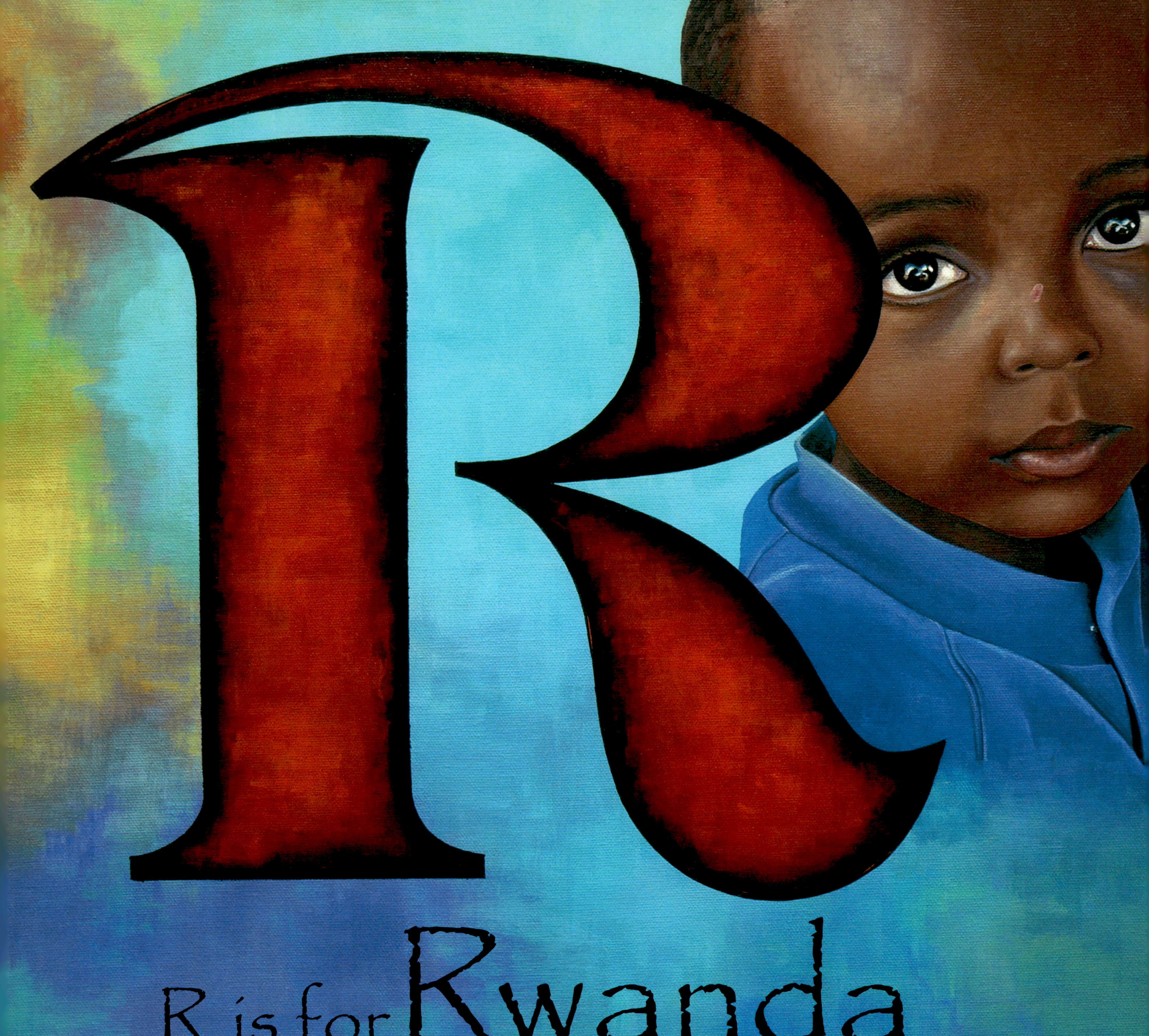

R is for Rwanda

The Cycle

Mama where are you?
Are you with my dad?
What did you and Daddy do?
Did you make them mad?

So many lives were taken.
Humanity in shame.
Survivors left to understand.
Governments to blame.

Mama, you have a grandson.
He is very shy.
His daddy died.
His mama's sick.
It hurts to see him cry.

The sickness has found me.
Soon I will be gone.
Another child all alone.
The cycle just goes on.

"Let us be the ones who say we do not accept that a child dies every three seconds simply because he does not have the drugs you and I have. Let us be the ones to say we are not satisfied that your place of birth determines your right to life. Let us be outraged, let us be loud, let us be bold."

–Brad Pitt, Actor

About "The Cycle"

TERRIFIED CHILDREN, screaming and running from the gruesome scene of their parents' murders, some reaching safety, others being gunned down in their tracks…none returning to their childhoods…ever:

This is the reality of what took place in Rwanda during one of the worst massacres in history. It was a slaughter that lasted one hundred days and took the lives of over eight-hundred thousand people—a murderous rampage that left over ninety-five thousand children orphaned, and turned neighbors into killers. Ethnic differences determined life or death, innocence died, hatred exploded, and the future was forever changed for those left in its wake.

This is genocide, a word used to describe some of the darkest events in world history, a word that exudes blame, guilt and shame. Genocide is a word powerful enough to cause governments and politicians to dance nervously around it, afraid to acknowledge what it suggests, the evil it exposes, the human failure it identifies. Yet, the word "genocide" does not come close to conveying the pain and fear that children experience, children who are too young to comprehend but still endure its horrors. Nor does it provide justice or reparation to the victims who, after fourteen years, still struggle to find their place in the world. Traumatized and alone, the orphans of the massacre face another brutal killer. In addition to guns, machetes and grenades, rape was also a weapon of the Rwanda genocide. Widespread rape was used as a strategy to change the ethnic balance. It is estimated that between a quarter- to a half-million women and girls were raped during the hundred days of violence.

Today, the effects of this crime against humanity are clear. AIDS is claiming more lives in staggering numbers. Mothers are dying, leaving their orphaned children to fend for themselves. Babies are born under a death sentence in the form of the AIDS virus. The genocide of 1994 is still killing, more slowly, more quietly, but just as deadly.

It is abundantly clear that the international community failed the Rwandan people by allowing this tragic event to unfold. Today, the world has been given a second chance to step in and stop the suffering. We have the opportunity to protect these children from the silent killer left behind.

Medication, health care and education: these are life-saving tools the world can give to the children of Rwanda. Hope and healing are all that they have to cling to. As Gandhi said, "I have seen children successfully surmounting the effects of an evil inheritance. That is due to purity being an inherent attribute of the soul."

Who are these children who need our help? They are the children who witnessed the unleashing of grown-up hatred and prejudices, the children who saw their parents and siblings slaughtered, the children who were raped and now face certain death of a slower kind, the children who were orphaned, and the children who participated in the killings, too young to know better. All of them deserve the protection and compassion that the world once failed to give them.

Did you know… Approximately eighteen percent of all children under the age of eighteen are orphans in Rwanda?

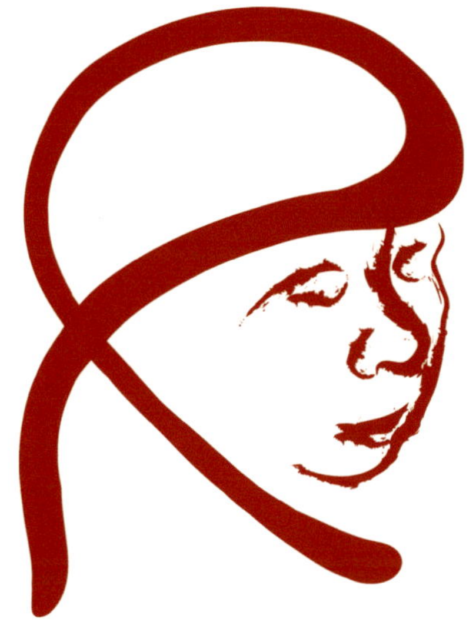

FACE AIDS

A student campaign to fight AIDS in Africa

"Young people often bear the brunt of the devastating impact of HIV/AIDS. I applaud FACE AIDS for their leadership in engaging youth from around the world on this pandemic, and am pleased that FACE AIDS is supporting my Foundation's collaboration with Partners In Health in Rwanda."

–President William J. Clinton

What We Believe

We believe in a simple fact: AIDS is a preventable and treatable disease. Yet in 2007 more than two million people died from AIDS, the majority of whom lived in sub-Saharan Africa. AIDS continues to take lives, devastate families, and undermine entire societies due to the lack of basic resources, medicine, and interventions to fight the disease. We believe that with a broad-based social commitment

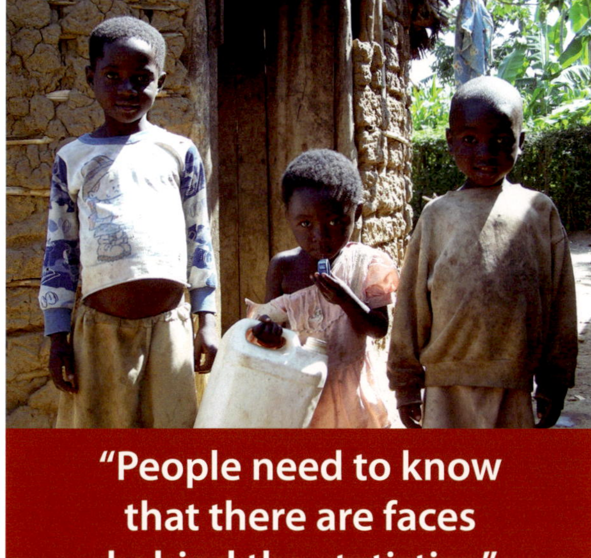

"People need to know that there are faces behind the statistics."

we have the ability to address this tragedy and to close the gap between what we are capable of accomplishing medically, and what we have thus far accomplished socially. We seek to inspire young people to fight the AIDS pandemic in Africa, and to build a student movement behind the idea that individuals should not die of a preventable and treatable disease simply because they were born into a situation of poverty.

For many young people in the U.S., AIDS is a huge, scary, anonymous problem. News stories focus on millions of deaths and orphans, on huge scientific challenges, and on policy failings. These are great tragedies. But people need to know that there are faces behind the statistics. There are lives in the numbers. And they need to know that these lives do not need to be lost, and that where there are tragedies there are also solutions.

What We Do

FACE AIDS spreads this message of humanity and hope to future leaders through our college and high school chapters across the United States.

To inspire our peers to commit to this issue, FACE AIDS chapters at over 150 colleges and high schools nationwide work to put a human face on the pandemic. FACE AIDS campus campaigns center around the distribution of AIDS Awareness Pins made by men and women affected by AIDS who work in income generating support groups in rural Rwanda.

When students receive the pins they also receive the name, picture, and story of the individual pin-maker. They learn about the hopes and dreams of the man or woman living with AIDS, or caring for a child with AIDS. They learn about the daily challenges he or she faces, and the courage it takes to overcome illness and stigma. Most importantly, they learn to see the faces of AIDS, not just the numbers.

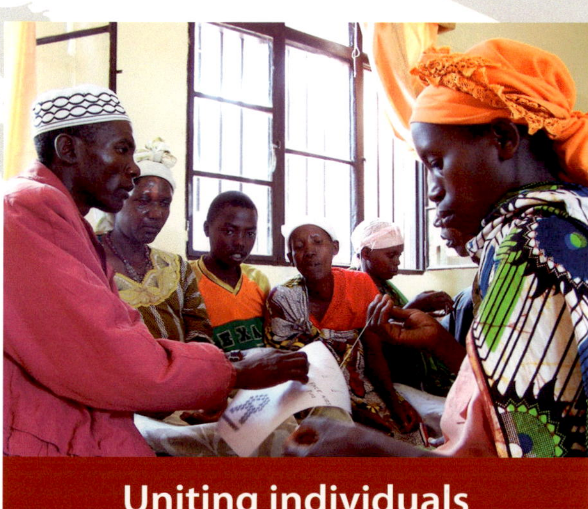

Uniting individuals to fight the pandemic.

To show our peers that we can address this tragedy, FACE AIDS connects students to the best organization treating AIDS and providing comprehensive health care in poor countries, Partners In Health. All money raised by FACE AIDS chapters is paired with matching grants from private donors and given to support Partners In Health's clinics in Rwanda. In just two years, through the inspirational work of students and donors across the United States, we have engaged tens of thousands of young people, and raised over $1 million for this fight.

Join the movement • Start, join, or support the chapter at your school • www.faceaids.org

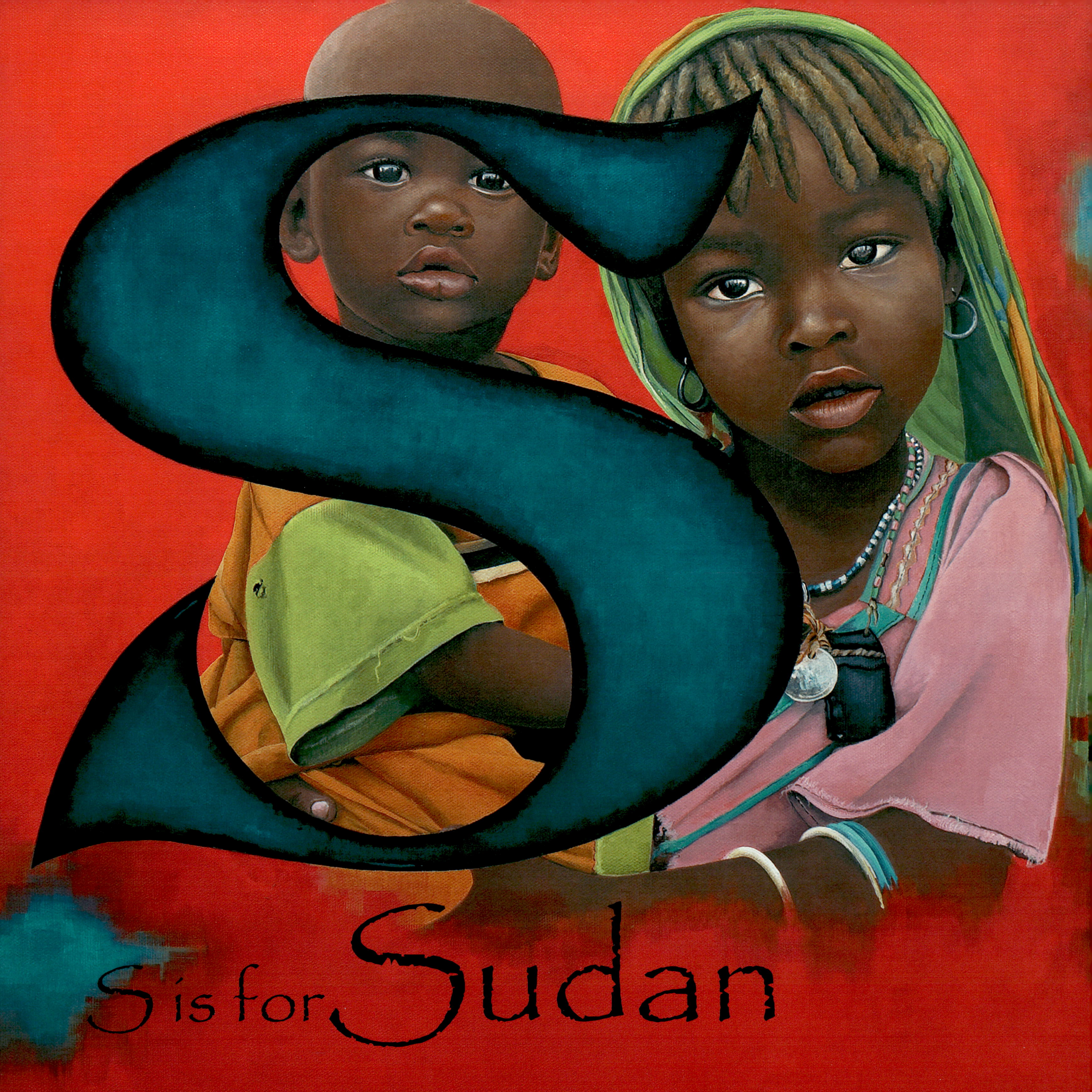
S is for Sudan

In The End

The fear is like a knife
That hovers overhead.
It's with us in the morning
And when we go to bed.

I see the people dying.
Children weep and cry.
I see the soldiers killing.
I want to ask them why.

I hear the word genocide.
Please tell me what it means.
Does it mean that we are bad,
Less than human beings?

That we deserve to die
Just because of race,
The things that we believe in,
Or the color of our face?

That lives can be taken
Cultures wiped away?
That children sit in camps
Too afraid to play?

When will people figure out
That killing isn't right?
That in the end, no one wins,
No matter what the fight.

"If nations are allowed to commit genocide with impunity, to hide their guilt in a camouflage of lies and denials, there is real danger that other brutal regimes will be encouraged to attempt genocides."

–Caroline, Baroness Cox, House of Lords

About "In the End"

HOW MANY RED FLAGS, debates and headlines will it take? How many people need to die before we recognize genocide prior to it becoming a dark shadow in the annals of world history? After a shameful admission of our "failure to respond" to the atrocities committed in Cambodia and Rwanda, and a promise of "never again", the world looked to the UN as children would look to a parent who has disappointed them. Formed after World War II, the UN was designed to be an international watch dog, constructed to defend humanity and to prevent the future from ever resembling the past. So what has gone wrong? Is the watchdog asleep…again?

One of the first people to recognize what is occurring in Darfur as genocide is a man named Eric Reeves. At the time, he was not a political expert, a UN watchdog, a journalist or activist; instead, he was a college English professor whose observations of the situation did not sit well with him. He refuted under-estimates of the death toll and crunched the numbers himself. While most reports whispered that thousands were dying in a civil war, he shouted that tens of thousands were dying in a campaign of ethnic cleansing.

His outcry, his refusal to let a single death go unaccounted for, has become the driving force behind the Save Darfur Movement, which has saved hundreds of thousands of lives; impressive and frustrating. If one man in an unrelated career can do so much, why is more not being done by the international community? It is hard to believe that anyone would argue that what's been happening in Darfur over the past four years is anything but genocide. Yet, the United States is the only governing body that has dared to admit the truth.

We have an obligation to stop the genocide taking place in Sudan. The death toll continues to rise and by Eric Reeves' estimates (he is now considered an expert) it may have reached five hundred thousand in overall conflict related deaths. This toll could skyrocket if measures are not effectively taken to protect the two and a half million people currently displaced. The complexity of the situation in Sudan challenges even experts as it spans decades and involves a cast of political characters, rebel militias, propaganda and theories of roots and causes too numerous for the average person to conceive, let alone comprehend.

Instead of getting lost in the vast amount of information, time lines and details leading up to and surrounding the crisis, perhaps we should each decide for ourselves what we will tolerate. After all, we each share this world, and in doing so have both a right and an obligation to determine for ourselves when enough is enough. We are not individually or collectively bound by any law to wait patiently for the bureaucratic powers that be to tell us what we already know in our hearts, what we already see with our own eyes. We are witnessing genocide.

We cannot continue to rely on a watchdog that is prone to taking too long to identify the danger. We cannot fall back on the many excuses we use to explain our complacency. We know it's happening. It's happening in real time, while we work, while we sleep and while we find ways to avoid knowing more or feeling more.

We can blame governments, they make easy targets. We can blame the media, yet we consume whatever they feed us. We can blame evil forces that answer to no one, like the Janjaweed rebel militia carrying out genocide on the people of Darfur. In the end, if we don't act, if we don't respond, we must also blame ourselves.

Did you know… Since 2003, in the Darfur region of Sudan, over four hundred thousand people have been killed and over two million have been displaced?

ABOUT ENOUGH
OUR STORY

Born out of frustration and hope.

We ran out of patience with the world's shameful lack of progress in combating terrible horrors, but knew there were many examples of successful conflict resolution, but the lessons weren't widely known. We found confidence in the growing number of Americans who are demanding more aggressive, successful solutions.

ENOUGH aims to answer questions about what is really happening and offer a clear path to sustainable solutions. We started in early 2007, setting out to establish a new paradigm for action.

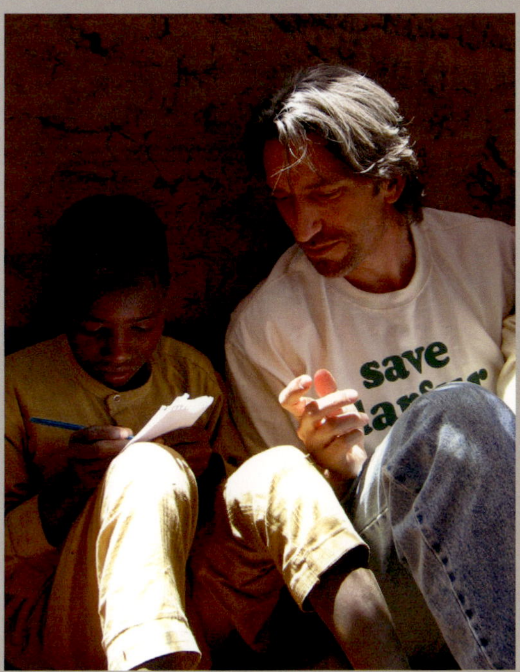

ENOUGH Co-Founder John Prendergast with a refugee in Chad, June 2nd, 2006

We aim for real change to close the book on these horrible recurring chapters of human history.

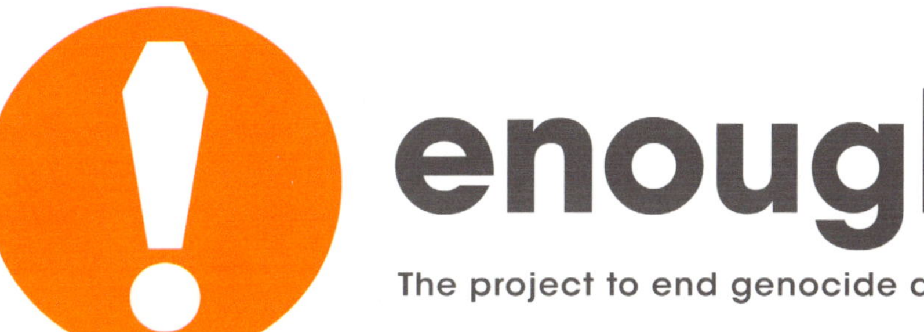

The project to end genocide and crimes against humanity

OUR APPROACH

PEACE + PROTECTION + PUNISHMENT

There is no silver bullet to eradicate genocide and crimes against humanity. But with hard work, dedication, and help from others, ENOUGH has examined successful cases of conflict resolution throughout Africa and found that there are almost always three ingredients to success.

Promote Peace

Building peace costs less – in lives and in dollars – than picking up the pieces after a humanitarian crisis. The best way to end genocide and mass atrocities is with persistent, high-level diplomacy aimed at creating sustainable peace and laying the groundwork for a secure future.

Provide Protection

Even as we pursue peace, we must protect innocent people persecuted by genocidal violence and destructive instability. ENOUGH identifies and pushes for actions that the United States and its partners must take to protect a country's citizens from crimes against humanity when their government can or will not.

Punish Perpetrators

We must hold the perpetrators of these crimes accountable, during and after atrocities. To break the cycle of impunity, we must impose substantive consequences on those who commit these crimes and on those who provide support.

TAKE ACTION ON SUDAN

Lead Your Leaders by Contacting the White House.

Ask the Candidates what they will do as President to stop violence in Darfur, ensure the success of the Comprehensive Peace Agreement in southern Sudan, and prevent future genocide and crimes against humanity.

Support Divestment Efforts. Since 2005, 20 states and over 50 universities have adopted Sudan divestment policies. Are your investments supporting the Sudanese regime? Are your leaders?

Read "Not on Our Watch: The Mission to End Genocide in Darfur and Beyond" by Don Cheadle and John Prendergast.

Are you doing ENOUGH? www.enoughproject.org

ENOUGH Project • 1225 Eye Street NW, Suite 307 • Washington DC 20005 • www.enoughproject.org

T is for Tibet

Begging to Understand

I have some questions
I'd like to ask,
Some things I'd like to know.
Why'd they make us leave our home?
Where'd they think we'd go?

Who is sleeping in our house,
While we sleep on the street?
How come I have to beg
For the little food I eat?

Why is the ground so hard?
Why are the nights so cold?
Why is there a fee for school,
That Tibetans can't afford?

Why are people being killed?
Who listens when children cry?
Why is the government doing this
And telling the world a lie?

Think about these questions.
I'd really like to know.
What's happening to Tibet,
And where are we to go?

The Heart of a Monk

In your efforts to remove us
You only proved us right.
That the heart of a monk
Is stronger than your might.

You've been brutal in your battle.
You even took our land.
But the peace within our hearts
You'll never understand.

You've been clever in your tactics.
So many people fooled.
Proving all your power
Over people that you've ruled.

But you cannot rule our hearts.
Did you know this to be true?
You can't take our faith away
When you beat us black and blue.

Yes, you've hurt us deeply.
This we won't deny.
You've forced your ways upon us
And told the world a lie.

But still we will not question
The things we know are right.
To coexist in harmony.
The conviction not to fight.

"Nonviolence is the greatest force at the disposal of mankind. It is mightier than the mightiest weapon of destruction devised by the ingenuity of man."

–Gandhi, Religious Leader

About "Begging to Understand" and "The Heart of a Monk"

A GOVERNMENT demonstrating absolute power and control over its people, is a recurring theme seen again and again throughout history. Corruption, greed and politics that exclude minorities, religious beliefs and basic human rights often lead these governments down a path of destruction. In their wake, shattered lives, ruined communities and lost cultures are sometimes all that remain. Before this process of destruction completes itself, there are opportunities for the international community to voice its objection; to emphatically say, "This is not okay." If such opposition goes unspoken, then future generations will only have books and photographs to remind them of some of the world's most beautiful lands and cultures.

Tibet, the highest occupied territory on earth, is at that pivotal point of salvation or destruction. Prior to 1949, Tibet was its own country with its own flag, currency, culture and religion based on an appreciation of all living things and the coexistence of humanity living in peace and tolerance. After the 1949, invasion of Tibet by the People's Liberation Army of China, the Chinese government began a communist rule. Since then, China has waged an ongoing campaign against Tibetans to infuse their culture with atheist views and to restrict the practice of their sacred religion, Buddhism. The government has also forbidden reference to and recognition of Tibet's true religious leader, the Dalai Lama.

After an uprising in 1959, by the Tibetan people, the Dalai Lama was forced to flee the country (he remains in exile today). More than eighty thousand Tibetans followed him, and tens of thousands who remained were killed or imprisoned. The exact number of Tibetans who have died through starvation, torture and execution as a result of China's rule will likely never be known. However, it is believed that this number is in the hundreds of thousands.

Today, the reins are being tightened even more over the Tibetans remaining in the region, and the strong arm tactics of yesterday have been abandoned for a more calculated strategy. While China tries to portray an interest and commitment to the well-being of the people of Tibet, the truth contradicts these theatrics. Tibetan's have been moved off their land, out of their homes, forced to give up their businesses and reduced to life threatening poverty. Freedom of speech and religious practice no longer exist in Tibet. Though China has rebuilt thousands of monasteries destroyed in the invasion, every activity and gathering held within these sacred locations is monitored by the Chinese police. Determined to control their religion, the government kidnapped one of Tibet's most adored figures, the Panchan Lama, second in holiness only to the Dalai Lama. At the time he was taken, he was only six years old, and as of today his whereabouts are unknown. In his place they selected a child whom they installed into a leadership position in a ceremony most Tibetan's consider a sham. Since then, the boy has been groomed by the government to one day have the privilege, if not the religious right, to select the next Dalai Lama.

While some wait in earnest for his holiness to return to Tibet, others have rebelled against the region's historical stance for peace and have begun responding with violence, playing right into China's strategy–a strategy that waits for Tibetans to lose faith. From his home in India, the Dalai Lama maintains his resilient posture against brutality and force. However, his faith alone cannot restore their freedom. Voices from around the world, speaking in unison and taking action are the only hope for saving Tibet.

Did you know... In Tibet, worshipping the Dalai Lama is a crime punishable by imprisonment?

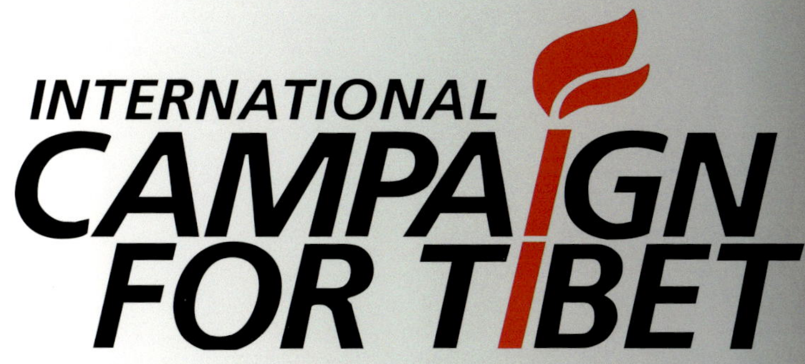

"Our prime purpose in life is to help others. And if you can't help them at least don't hurt them."

–Dalai Lama

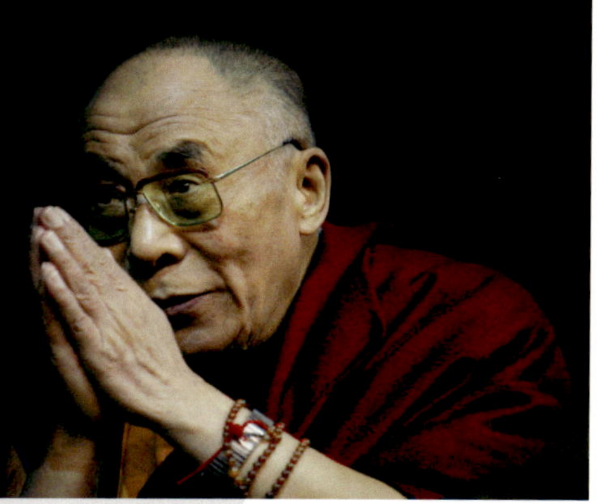

Our Mission is Freedom

At ICT, we fundamentally believe that there must be a political solution based on direct dialogue between the Dalai Lama and his representatives and the People's Republic of China. Without a negotiated solution for Tibet, China will never legitimize its role there. Moreover, to ensure peace and stability in the region, Tibetans must feel that their rights as a people have been acknowledged and understood.

ICT has a 20-year record of achievement advancing the Tibetan cause – and the vision and leadership of the Dalai Lama – in the halls of Congress and in international forums. We strive to mobilize international goodwill in support of the Tibetan people. Our focus today is centered on working with governments to demonstrate meaningful support for Tibet, reaching out to Chinese all over the world, and monitoring conditions inside Tibet.

And our message to Tibetans is to encourage even more dialogue about how foreign governments, NGOs, news outlets and others can better improve conditions in Tibet. In short, we are keeping our focus on Tibet and working to build trust, relationships and concrete improvements at the same time we work to invigorate international diplomatic efforts for Tibet.

The International Campaign for Tibet works to promote human rights and democratic freedoms for the people of Tibet by:

- **Monitoring and reporting** on human rights, environmental and socioeconomic conditions in Tibet.
- **Being advocates** for Tibetans imprisoned for their political or religious beliefs.
- **Working with governments** to develop policies and programs to help Tibetans.
- **Securing humanitarian and development assistance** for Tibetans.
- **Mobilizing individuals and the international community** to take action on behalf of Tibetans.
- **Promoting self-determination** for the Tibetan people through negotiations between the Chinese government and the Dalai Lama.

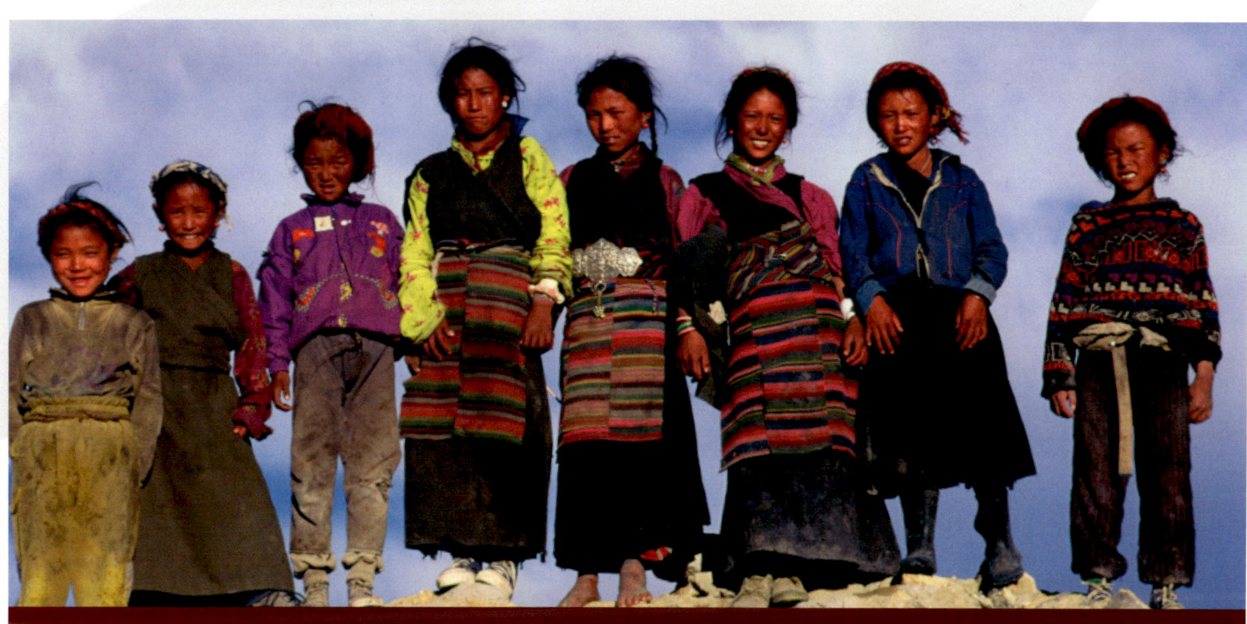

Our Message is Peace

"Tibet has a precious culture based on principles of wisdom and compassion. This culture addresses what we lack in the world today; a very real sense of inter-connectedness. We need to protect it for the Tibetan people, but also for ourselves and our children."

–Richard Gere, Chairman of the Board
International Campaign for Tibet

International Campaign For Tibet • 1825 Jefferson Place NW • Washington, DC 20036 • www.savetibet.com

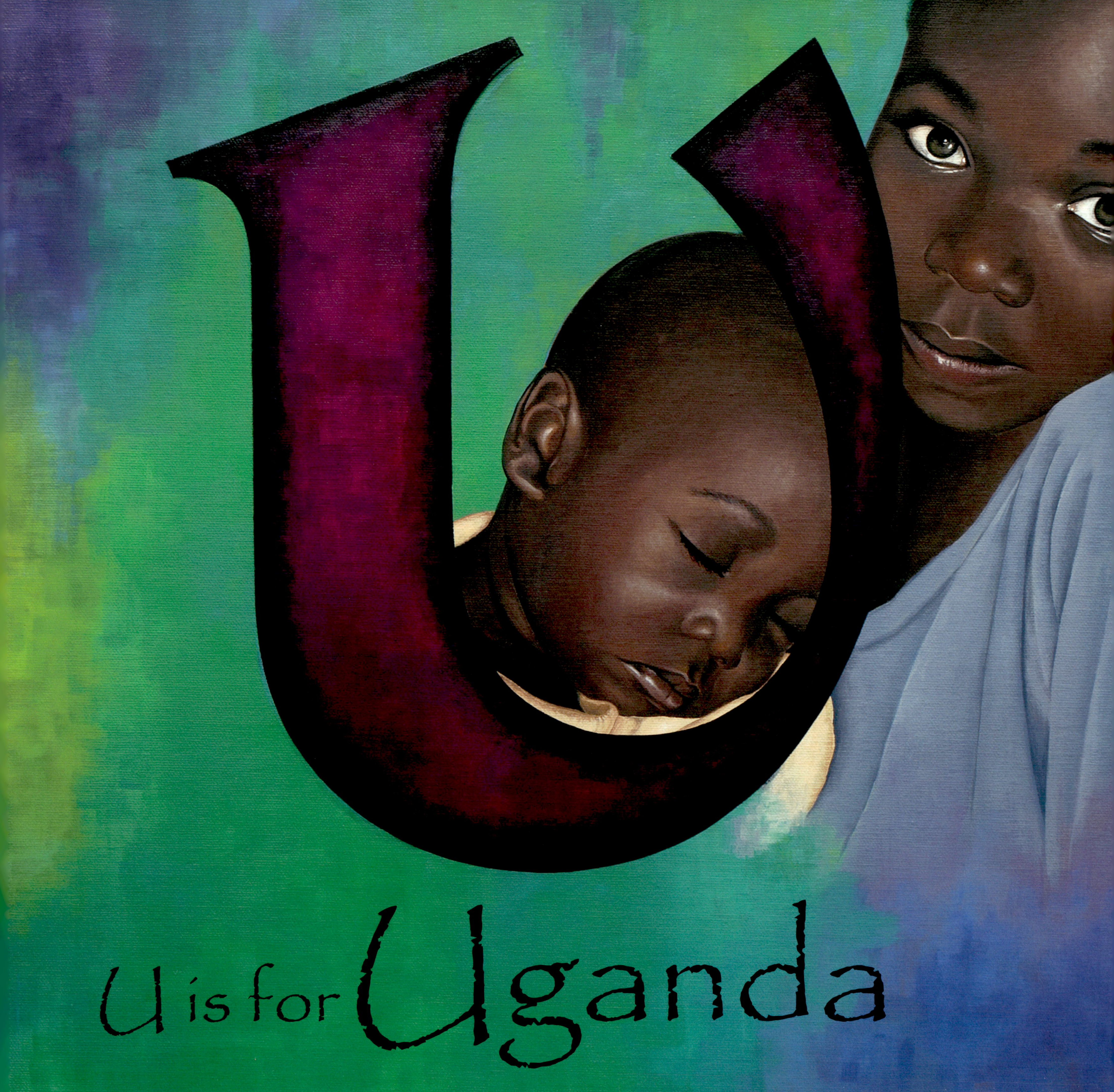
U is for Uganda

Night Terrors

I hold tight my sister's hand
As we make the walk each night,
Trying not to be abducted,
Abused and forced to fight.

When we find a place to sleep,
We curl up on the ground,
Fighting off the nightmares
Of what will happen if we're found.

We know the one's they take
Viciously trained to kill.
Children not yet old enough
To understand the blood they spill.

The lucky live another day
In fear and constant fright,
Again I'll hold my sister's hand
On that lonely road tonight.

"Compelled to become instruments of war, to kill and be killed, child soldiers are forced to give violent expression to the hatred of adults."

–Olara Otunnu, Special Representative Children and Armed Conflict, UN

About "Night Terrors"

THE WAR in northern Uganda has been called the most neglected humanitarian emergency in the world today. For over twenty-one years, an ongoing conflict between the government of Uganda and the Lord's Resistance Army (LRA), has left nearly two million innocent civilians caught in the middle and has produced an entire generation that has never known peace. Initially, the uprising against the government had significant support from the Ugandan people.

When Joseph Kony became the LRA's leader, bringing with him extreme tactics, support from the Ugandan people dwindled. It became a common practice of the LRA to fortify their ranks by abducting children and forcing them to become part of the LRA militia through indoctrination and dehumanization.

The children, stolen from their homes, villages, and schools, were often forced to kill a family member or friend as part of this process. The boys became soldiers trained to kill, and the girls were violated by the army's leaders and abused as child brides and servants. Why abduct children? They are small, moldable, require very little food and will do whatever is requested to avoid beatings and abuse.

As this practice of abduction pervaded northern Uganda, children of all ages, boys and girls, were forced to either leave their homes at night or risk being taken. The pilgrimage of thousands of children has been documented in video and photographs as they walked the many miles from their villages each night hoping to find a safe haven. If they were lucky, they were rewarded with a few hours of fearful sleep before making the trek back the next morning. These children became known as "night commuters".

In 1996, in response to the LRA attacks in the villages, the Ugandan government forcibly evicted thousands from their homes and relocated them into overcrowded camps in hopes of providing protection. In 2002, the number of child "night commuters" was estimated to be over twenty-five thousand. Since peace talks began between the LRA and the Uganda Government in 2006, night commuting has all but ceased. While this should give us great hope, this hope should keep company with grave concern for the Ugandans still crowded into camps in the North. Over a decade after these camps were created, roughly one and a half million individuals remain and struggle to survive among the effects of abject poverty, rampant disease, and near-certain starvation.

Until a peace agreement is reached, and until the aftermath is fully addressed by holding the perpetrators accountable for their crimes against humanity, children in Uganda will remain in jeopardy at the center of this crisis. We cannot let the children continue to suffer. We must protect their rights, and we must partner to rehabilitate them and their communities. None of us can undo past evils or the scars that they leave, but we can help the children of Uganda to move forward. We can help to rebuild their trust. We can help to educate them to be better leaders tomorrow than we have today. We can give them back the ability to dream, and at the very least, the ability to sleep without fear.

Did you know... It has been estimated that over ninety percent of the Lord's Resistance Army has been made up of children?

Invisible children

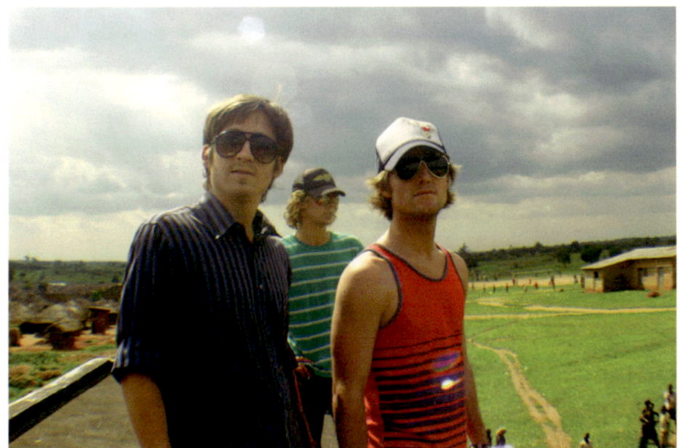

How It All Began

In the spring of 2003 three young filmmakers-Jason Russell, Bobby Bailey and Laren Poole-traveled to Africa in search of a story.

What started out as a filmmaking adventure transformed into much more when these boys from Southern California discovered a tragedy that disgusted and inspired them, a tragedy where children are both the weapons and the victims.

After returning to the States they created the documentary "Invisible Children: Rough Cut," a film that exposes the tragic realities of northern Uganda's night commuters and child soldiers.

The film was originally shown to friends and family, but has now been seen by millions of people. The overwhelming response has been, "How can I help?" To answer this question the nonprofit Invisible Children, Inc. was created, giving compassionate individuals an effective way to respond to the situation.

Who We Are

We are storytellers. We are visionaries, humanitarians, artists, and entrepreneurs. We are individuals part of a generation eager for change and willing to pursue it.

As a nonprofit we work to transform apathy into activism. By documenting the lives of those living in regions of conflict and injustice, we hope to educate and inspire individuals in the Western world to use their unique voice for change. Our media creates an opportunity for people to become part of a grassroots movement that intelligently responds to what's happening in the world.

But our work extends beyond our borders. In war-affected regions we focus on long-term development, working directly with individuals and institutions that are eager to realize their full potential. Through education and innovative economic opportunities, we partner with affected communities and strive to improve the quality of life for individuals living in conflict and post-conflict regions.

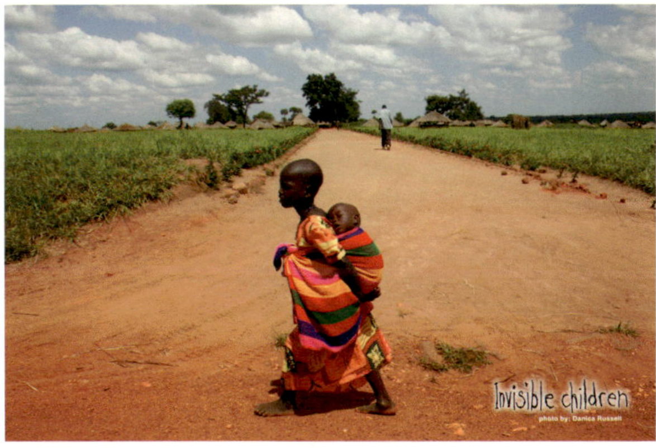

"Invisible Children is a movement that has forced me to act."
–Kristen Bell, Actor, Heroes

How We Make a Difference

Our approach to humanitarian work is founded in the strength and intelligence of the Ugandan community. We learned early on it was not only important but essential to heed the wisdom of people that had not only lived in the war, but were surviving it. People who would know better than anyone what the greatest needs were and the best ways to meet them. What we came to find is that while there have been many efforts to address the issues that stem from living and fighting in such a long-lasting war, the people of Uganda are asking for a future beyond the conflict.

Their pleas have become our development strategy.

All of our programming is a partnership between those of us at Invisible Children and those in the Ugandan community. We focus on long-term goals that enable children to take responsibility for their future and the future of their country. Our programs are carefully researched and developed initiatives that address the need for quality education, mentorships, the redevelopment of schools, resettlement from the camps, and financial stability.

"If you want to know how to change the world, see Invisible Children.*"*
–Shadyac, Director, Bruce Almighty

Can a Story Change the World?... It Already Has.

Invisible Children, Inc. • 2705 Via Orange Way, Suite B • Spring Valley, CA 91978 • www.invisiblechildren.com

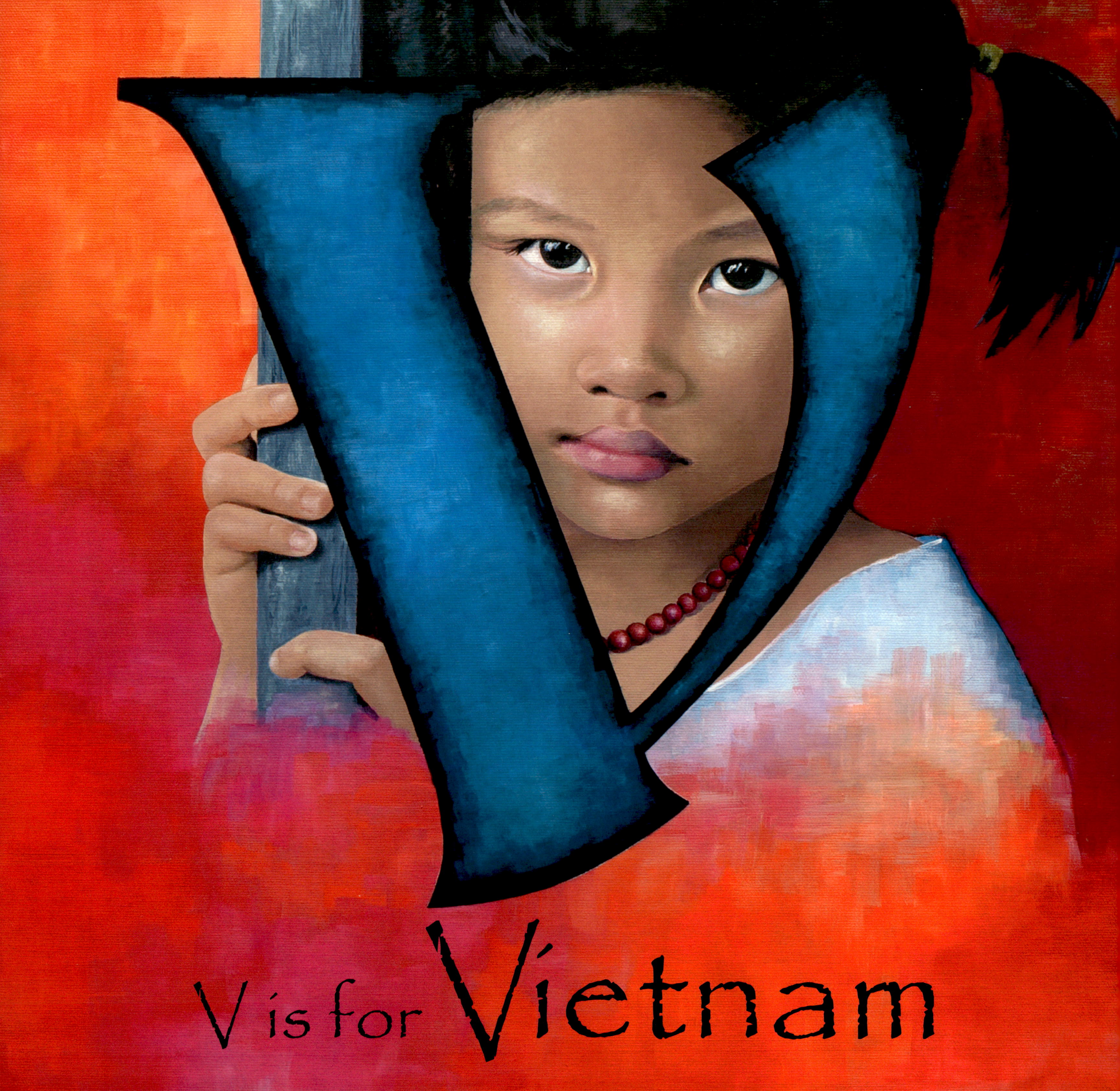
V is for Vietnam

The Child I Was

Why do these men come in
And do the things that hurt?
I don't like the way it feels
Their hands beneath my skirt.

I know what they are doing
Is wrong and very bad.
But I do as I'm told,
It's worse when they get mad.

Once they leave I curl up
My companions: shame and fear.
My cheek is wet and dirty
From the falling of a tear.

I hear another child scream.
I'm not the only one.
Cover my ears, close my eyes.
I wish that I could run.

I think about the child I was.
I dream of going home.
He's here again. I open my eyes.
Oh God, he's not alone!

"The time has come to make the protection of children–all our children–a common cause that can unite us across the boundaries of our political orientation, religious affiliation and cultural traditions. We must reclaim our lost taboos and make the abuse and brutalization of children simply unacceptable."

–Olara Otunnu, Special Representative Children and Armed Conflict, UN

About "The Child I Was"

A FIVE-YEAR-OLD GIRL, dressed in cotton paisley pajamas, rubbing the sleep from her eyes with one tiny balled up fist; an image of innocence and vulnerability. Is there anything more priceless than the beauty of a child just returning from the peacefulness of sleep?

For those lacking a conscience and the emotions that separate humans from other species, this isn't a priceless image. Tragically, in places around the globe, little girls are offered up like items on a menu, the price of innocence sometimes less than a bottle of beer. If your moral compass is working, you will find this difficult to believe. Unfortunately, it is an appalling truth that we need to acknowledge.

Cambodia has long been a hot bed for those looking for entertainment that expends the innocence of children without regard for their dignity or human rights. Just across the border, Vietnam supplies the vast majority of this commodity into the Cambodian market. The pressures of an exploding population, extreme poverty and government corruption are responsible for condemning an alarming number of girls into this horrific nightmare. Opportunistic individuals and criminal organizations thrive on the marginalized conditions facing the Vietnamese people, and those in positions of authority choose to look the other way. Throw in the perverse appetite of a group of international consumers and you have places like Svay Pak in Cambodia, where girls of all ages lose not only their freedom but their souls and often their lives.

These are young children who have been taken from their homes, sometimes sold by their own parents into a world darker than their worst nightmares. Forced to have sex every day with countless strangers, they are routinely beaten, tortured and fed narcotics to which they become addicted. Little children–mostly girls, but sometimes boys–are sold into a life of physical abuse and mental anguish simply because there is a profit to be made and twisted pleasure to be had. This is without question one of most disturbing human rights violations occurring in our world today.

Unfortunately, and in spite of its incredulous nature, sex trafficking is a booming trend that defies all progress made in the arena of human rights. The numbers are staggering, the prevalence frightening and the price paid by each victim is heart wrenching. To imagine a little girl forced to suffer in this manner is almost incomprehensible. Nevertheless, we need to get our arms around it. This issue extends far beyond personal suffering. It is a major cause of the epidemic spread of AIDS. Studies show that the younger the victim, the higher the risk of contracting AIDS. The percentage of young victims testing positive for HIV/AIDS is shocking, and the threat of the virus spreading into other areas of the world is very real. Today there are places that boast as many as eighteen brothels on a single street. Places where laws mean nothing, because those who make them have more to gain by ignoring them then by enforcing them. Tourism, even the darkest kind, is what some countries thrive on. The issue is complex and not easily eradicated. It involves corruption at the highest levels, organized crime, socioeconomic factors, cultural indifference and an evil component of human nature that seems impervious to measures attempting to curb it.

Then, there are the children, the little girl in paisley pajamas rubbing the sleep from her eyes. This image alone mandates that in spite of every obstacle, a solution must be found so that these children can pursue the dreams they deserve to have.

Did you know… Vietnam is the number one source for trafficking children into Cambodia's sex trade?

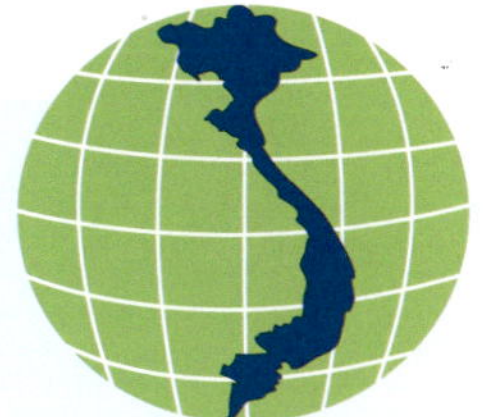

east meets west FOUNDATION

the foundation for learning, healing and health

Who We Are

The East Meets West Foundation (EMW) is "the foundation for learning, healing and health." EMW's work reflects the belief that every person should have access to clean water, proper medical treatment and a decent education. Without these fundamental elements of a good life, children cannot thrive and adults cannot be fully productive members of society. Founded in 1988, EMW has a 20-year track record of innovative and effective work in Vietnam and a vast portfolio of completed projects. EMW projects and programs are known for their high quality, long-term sustainability, emphasis on results, and significant scale.

Mission Statement

The East Meets West Foundation transforms the health, education and communities of disadvantaged people in Southeast Asia by building partnerships, developing opportunities and creating sustainable solutions.

Program Overview

The East Meets West Foundation's work falls under two main areas: we operate a variety of grassroots programs in Vietnam; and, we are active in building the infrastructure of the country through our Large Construction program.

Grassroots Programs

- **ADAPT**–the An Giang Dong Thap Alliance for the Prevention of Trafficking, a program jointly run by EMW, Pacific Links Foundation and International Children Assistance Network, works with a population of high at-risk girls in two southern provinces of Vietnam near the Cambodian border to prevent them from being sexually trafficked through scholarships, job training, and a strong community support network.
- **Breath of Life**–supplies hospitals in Vietnam with modern medical equipment and training to save the lives of premature infants and newborns.
- **School Construction Program**–builds primary schools and early childhood education centers in rural areas to close the education gap in Vietnam.
- **Clean Water and Sanitation Program**–provides access to safe water and good sanitation that is essential to leading a healthy and productive life.
- **Dental Program**–provides free, modern dental care to disadvantaged children through a state-of-the-art dental clinic in Da Nang, Outreach Trips that reach children in remote areas, and a mobile dental clinic.
- **Operation Healthy Heart**–gives critically ill children and their families funding and assistance for life-saving surgeries to treat congenital heart defects.
- **SPELL Program**–an innovative drop-out prevention initiative, provides scholarships for low-income children that follow them from third grade through high school.
- **Support Network for People with Disabilities**–creates channels of medical, educational, and vocational support for people with disabilities.
- **Village of Hope**–is a safe haven for 150 orphaned, disadvantaged, and deaf children in Da Nang.

Large Construction Projects

EMW invests in Vietnam's future through our large-scale building projects such as building hospitals, libraries, university facilities, bridges, dams and much more. Visit our web site to see a list of EMW large construction projects.

Help Us to Bring a Brighter Future to Families and Children of Vietnam!

East Meets West Foundation • PO Box 29292 • Oakland, CA 94604 • www.eastmeetswest.org • 800-561-3378

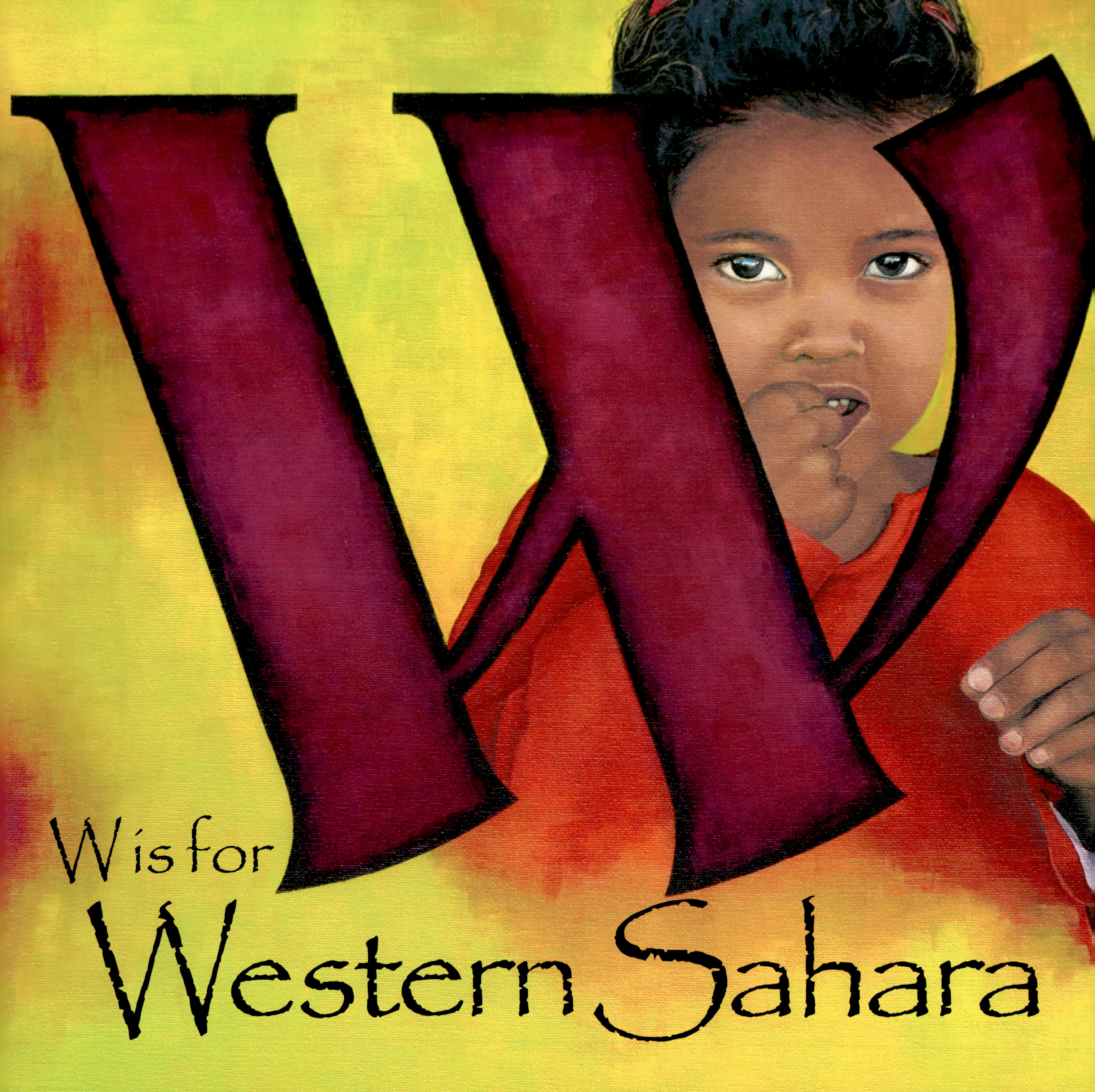
W is for
Western Sahara

Our Story

Do you know our story?
The injustice and the lies?
Have you ever tried to sleep
While a hungry baby cries?

A lonely life in exile.
A desert hot and dry.
Without the things we need
A lot of people die.

More than thirty years ago
Is when it all began.
Yet, we've been promised freedom
A hundred times since then.

Do you know our story?
The politics and greed?
Have you ever watched a child die
Without the help they need?

Do you know our story?
If you don't, I think you should.
I think the world would be ashamed
If they understood.

"In countries where people have to flee their homes because of persecution and violence, political solutions must be found, peace and tolerance restored, so that the refugees can return home."

–Angelina Jolie, Actress

About "Our Story"

HORACE, THE ROMAN POET, wrote "The mountains are in labor, and a mouse is brought forth." This amusing anecdote was delivered by retired U.S. Ambassador Frank Ruddy in a speech about his observations as the former Deputy Chairman for the United Nations Peacekeeping Mission in Western Sahara. Not so amusing is the political blunder, scandal and travesty of justice the rest of his presentation illuminated about the oldest territorial conflict in Africa.

In 1975, Morocco invaded Western Sahara, forcing most of the Sahrawi people into exile, where they remain today. This hostile land grab came the day after the World Court rejected Morocco's claim over the territory. Since then, in blatant defiance of a decision by the highest court on earth, Morocco has maintained an illegal occupation of Western Sahara, relegating most of the Sahrawi people to refugee camps in Algeria. In temperatures reaching over one hundred and twenty-two degrees in the summer and below freezing in the winter, the Sahrawi people struggle to survive in a place previously considered uninhabitable. Those who remain in the Moroccan occupied territory suffer abuses and systematic discrimination. Even peaceful demonstrations result in violence. The fate of the Sahrawi people and the disregard for justice should be of great concern to all of us, yet surprisingly few of us are aware of the situation.

For more than thirty-three years, Morocco has been given impunity while breaking international law. After fifteen years of simmering guerilla warfare between the Sahrawi military arm and the Moroccan army, a cease-fire was brokered between the two by the UN in 1991. The cease-fire was intended to lead to a referendum on self-determination.

The UN mission in Western Sahara known as MINURSO has operated at an estimated cost of one hundred thousand dollars a day since 1995. So far, more than one hundred UN Security Council and General Assembly resolutions have confirmed and reconfirmed the Sahrawi's right to self-determination. Morocco is not only in defiance of international law—they are conducting a campaign of terror. All of this is being carried out under the nose of a mission which was implemented to oversee justice. Human Rights Watch, based in New York, published a thirty-eight page report on MINURSO, which documented blatant human rights violations as well as voter fraud carried out by Morocco. Amnesty International reports disturbing incidences including forced disappearances, the use of torture during interrogations, detention of political activists, deportations, censorship and unfair trials.

Today, the Sahrawi people feel betrayed and forgotten. More than one hundred and sixty-five thousand Sahrawi's continue to live in exile. Because the camps are located in such an unforgiving climate, refugees rely entirely on outside aid for life-sustaining supplies such as food, water and medicine. Unfortunately, such aid has declined dramatically over the years and the situation is critical. Children are spending their lives as prisoners in life-threatening conditions. People are dying. The frustration is building and the potential for new bloodshed is real.

How many crimes need to be committed, how much evidence needs to be gathered, how much impunity will be given before the citizens in every country around the globe decide enough is enough? We need to care. We need to shake off our indifference, learn the facts and demand answers. Enough promises have been broken, and too many people continue to suffer.

Did you know... The Sahrawi people have been in exile for over thirty-three years through forced exodus by the Moroccan government under threat of extermination?

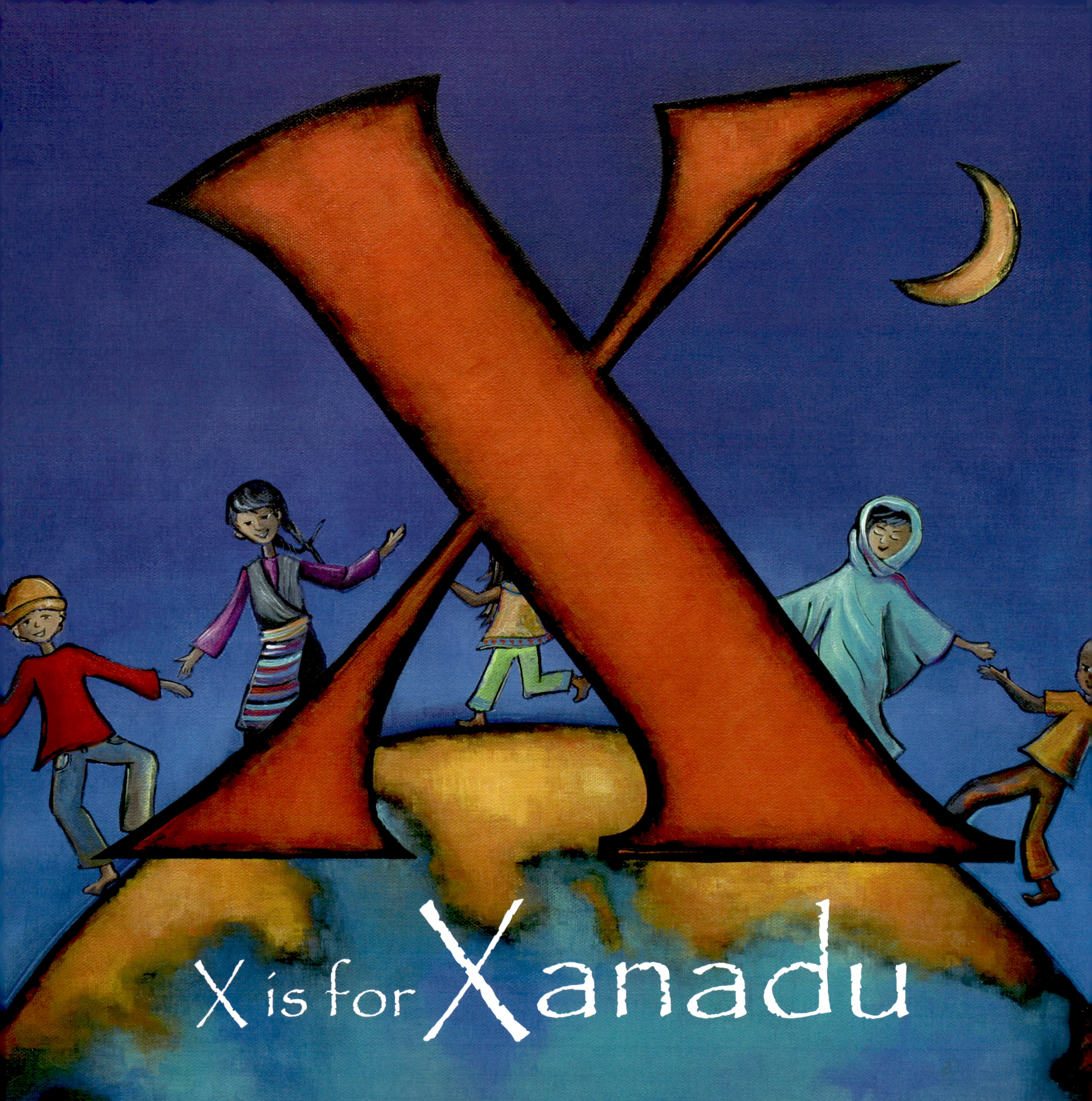
X is for Xanadu

What Could Be

I went to sleep last night,
Dreaming of a place,
Where children never cry,
And there is hope in every face.

A place where there's no poverty,
And people never fight.
A place where children sleep in beds
And have sweet dreams at night.

A place where every child thrives
And goes to school each day.
A place that isn't full of danger
When children go out to play.

A place where love is stronger
Than power, hate and greed.
A place where every child has
Exactly what they need.

Then I woke up this morning
And asked what I could do?
I've decided creating Xanadu
Starts with me and you.

"Our notion of the perfect society embraces the family as its center ornament, and this paradise is not secure until children appear to animate and complete the picture."

–Amos Bronson Alcot, American Educator and Social Reformer

About "What Could Be"

"XANADU" by definition means "a beautiful, idyllic place." What could be more beautiful than the concept of peace and equality in a climate of freedom and hope? A Pollyanna concept? Perhaps, but without ideals, without vision, we would live on the brink of absolute darkness with no impending dawn.

In complacency, we see tragedy as an unstoppable force, something that happens in spite of the most heroic efforts to waylay it. Given the frequency of horrific events occurring in our country, we are rarely shocked when tragedy occurs in other parts of the world. In many ways, the news has become predictable. Countries go to war; political unrest threatens the economy; poverty and AIDS simultaneously wipe out villages and communities; children are sold; impunity is bought; a child screams, and too often, the world hears nothing. Too many of us have become disheartened, believing that we are incapable, either alone or collectively, of defeating an army of human suffering. So we sit back, sometimes we watch, and almost always, we wait.

In a world that seems destined for shameful self-destruction, there is hope presented in the form of activism. Activism is a concept which was born from the idea that every voice can have impact, and the belief that a chorus of voices has infinite power. This concept does not recognize defeat in spite of all odds. Rather, it thrives on the simple idea that a pair of hands, an informed mind, a compassionate heart and an unbreakable conviction are as mighty as any weapons of destruction. Activism only works when people become active; individually and collectively. Simple laws of physics can be applied to this concept. If we succumb to complacency and do nothing, the outcome mirrors our efforts. If we do something, anything, the outcome, while unknown, has the potential to be better.

Optimism guides the activist when reality becomes blinding. It's not easy to address the images and stories about the children who suffer. Even more difficult is looking into the eyes of a child who is lost, afraid, hungry or sick, knowing that we may not have the answers. In the face of such overwhelming need, it is easier to hide amongst our personal comforts and to fill our lives with distractions that keep us from recognizing how little we are doing to improve humanity.

Each time one of us chooses to look instead of looking way, to speak out instead of bearing silent witness, and to stand up for the vulnerable against the corrupt, we are moving closer to changing the world. Each of us has a voice and an obligation to advocate freedom for those oppressed. Each of us has access to information so that we may become more informed, effective citizens in our world. Each of us has the ability to make a difference, even in the most discouraging conditions.

With knowledge comes culpability, and culpability demands action. When the discomfort begs us to look away, to change the channel, to put down the book, take another look and consider this: These are our children, our hope for a better future. Years from now, they will either be shining examples of the power of mankind's successes or evidence of complete human failure. To save humanity, we must save the children. There is no other way. "Xanadu" exists in the mind of every child. If we protect the children, if we watch them and learn from them, they will show us the way.

"Think of it. We are blessed with technology that would be indescribable to our forefathers. We have the wherewithal, the know-it-all to feed everybody, clothe everybody, and give every human on Earth a chance. We know now what we could never have known before–that we now have the option for all humanity to make it successfully on this planet in this lifetime. Whether it is to be Utopia or Oblivion will be a touch-and-go relay race right up to the final moment."

–Buckminster Fuller
Second President of Mensa

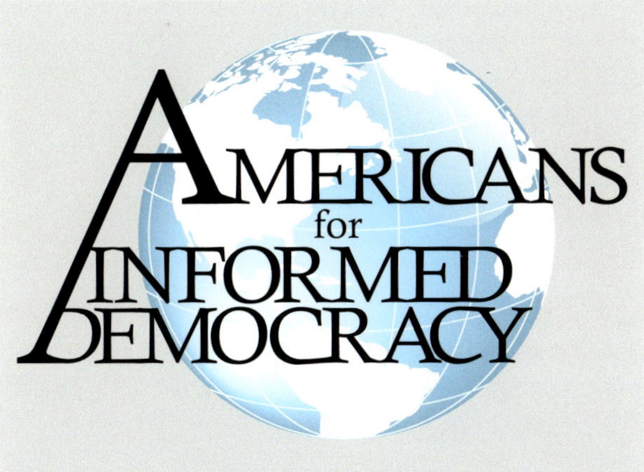

Awareness. Advocacy. Action.

Leaders of tomorrow...
creating change today.

Our organization has received recognition from highly regarded media and global institutions. Numerous editorial boards have praised our programs, including the Boston Globe, which called our Hope not Hate series "a victory of knowledge and inquiry over fear and blind pledges of revenge. This is public pressure at its noble best, able to cut through the haze of politics, inertia, and fear..." We received the 2005 Award for International Understanding from Search for Common Ground and were specially recognized by Madeleine Albright at the closing plenary session of the 2006 Clinton Global Initiative for our commitment to connecting young Americans with their peers.

AID empowers young people to create change locally on global issues. By connecting young people to policy experts, raising awareness, and providing the tools to create positive change, AID plays an instrumental role in building a more informed, equipped, and interconnected generation of young people who can press for positive U.S. foreign policy.

Helping Communities and Citizens Realize Their Future Promise

Young people have the optimism and global perspective to imagine a world where countries work together to end poverty, stop climate change, and eliminate terror. Many issues such as the environment, poverty, terrorism, and HIV/AIDS transcend national boundaries and affect young people here and abroad. Americans for Informed Democracy empowers young people to take up today's global challenges—such as climate change, poverty, AIDS, terrorism and violent conflict—as the special mission of their generation.

AID harnesses the unique energy and insight of young people to bring the world home to Americans and to showcase the opportunities for the U.S. to work with the international community to address global challenges that no nation alone can solve alone.

We work to raise young people's awareness of global issues, bring them potential solutions, connect them to foreign policy experts, host video-conference dialogues with students in other countries, and provide them with the tools to create positive change on their campuses, in their communities, and nationally.

Bringing People Together to Discuss Critical Issues

AID hosts conferences on critical global issues and brings together students and policy experts to dialogue and develop solutions. AID trains students to organize events on their campuses and develop campaigns to create local change. Our students have succeeded in getting their campuses to divest from Darfur, raised funds to buy bed nets to prevent malaria in Africa, and promote interfaith dialogue and programming on their campuses. AID informs students about how they can translate their concerns into policy change and connects them to U.S. policy solutions. AID students have succeeded in getting their communities to pass the Urban Environmental Accords—a UN backed plan for making communities more sustainable—and met with legislators on issues such as debt relief and education for youth in impoverished countries.

Working With Students on Campuses Globally

AID works with 23,000 students on more than 1,000 campuses nationwide to empower young leaders through our training retreats and conferences. Since 2002, our central organization has hosted more than 100 young global leaders summits in over 30 U.S. states and in six foreign countries to engage young leaders from Bob Jones University to Berkeley in our mission.

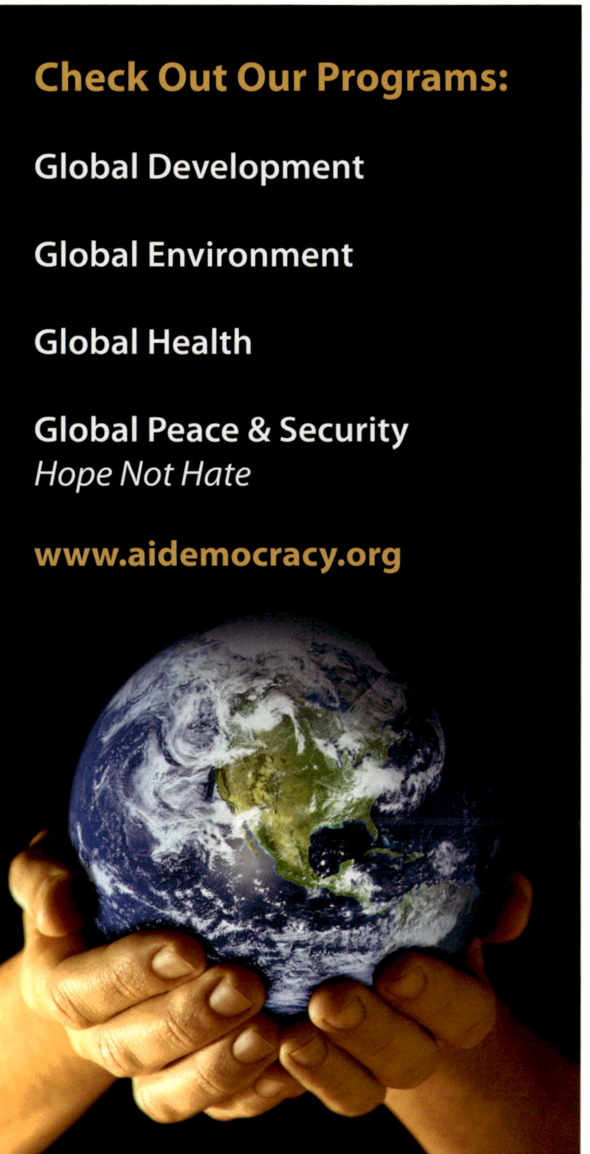

Americans for Informed Democracy • 701 Cathedral Street, Suite L3 • Baltimore, MD 21201 • www.aidemocracy.org

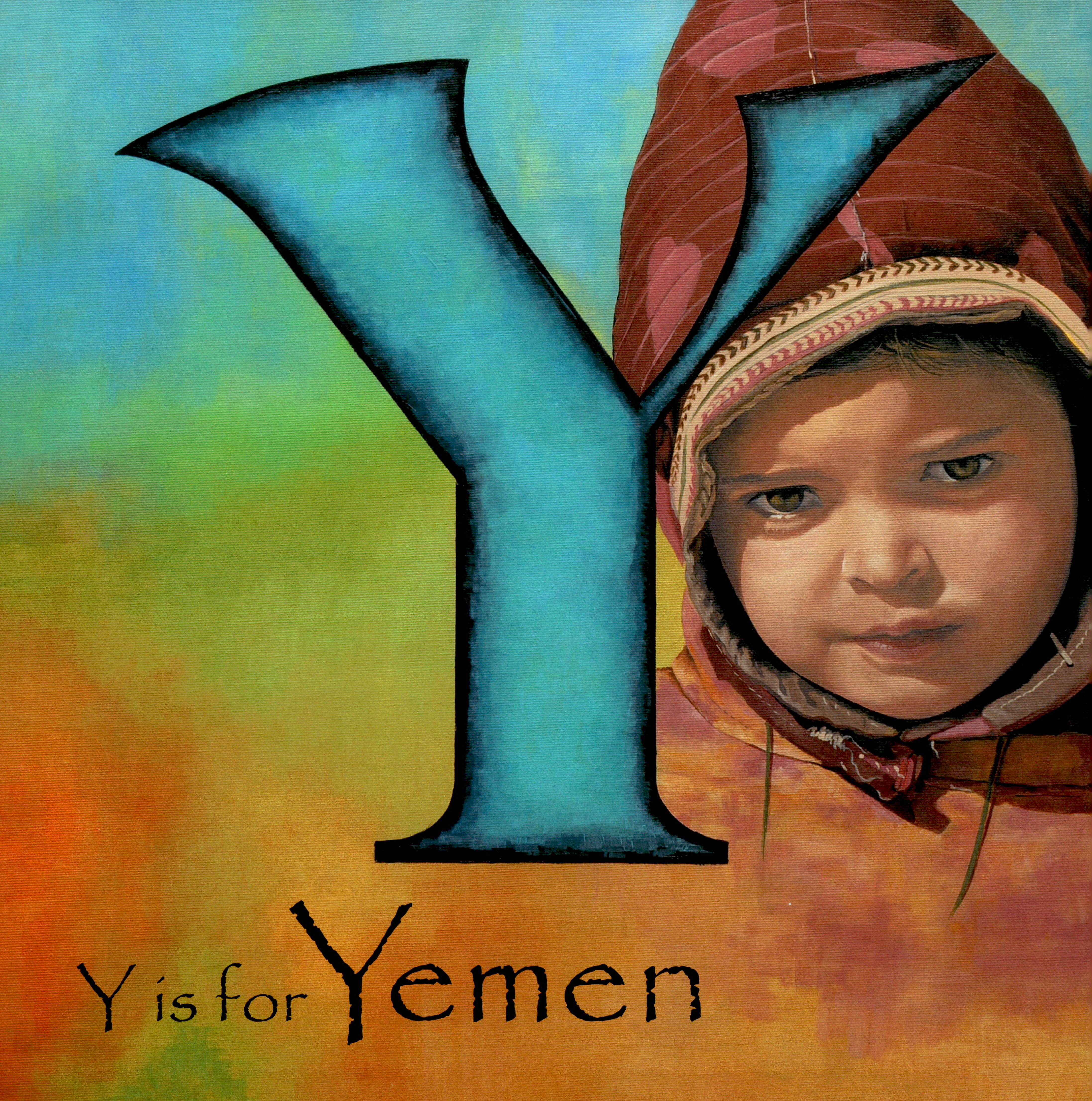
Y
Y is for Yemen

Abandoned and Betrayed

They told me we needed money,
And that I would have to go
Across the border to find work
With these men they know.

I was scared and really sad,
But did as I was told.
I don't know what work I'll do.
I'm only five years old.

They taught me how
To beg for money,
From people on the street.
They said if I didn't do it right
I wouldn't get to eat.

Even though I try real hard,
I always make them mad.
Then they do bad things to me.
I want my mom and dad.

"Child labor and poverty are inevitably bound together and if you continue to use the labor of children as the treatment for the social disease of poverty, you will have both poverty and child labor to the end of time."

–Grace Abbott, American Social Reformer, Teacher and Writer

About "Abandoned and Betrayed"

"HAVE MERCY on your small children who work in the streets with the heat of the sun, our childhood lost by the injustice of those older than us." These are some of the lyrics sung by a group of Yemeni children at a workshop focusing on children's rights. Their message and desperate call upon their parents to consider their anguish is unmistakable.

Yemen is another country suffering the many evils born of poverty. Half of Yemen's twenty-one million inhabitants are children. Forty-three percent of the entire population lives in poverty due to unemployment, inflation, socioeconomic status and government instability. The country's deteriorating economic condition is directly responsible for the inability of forty-five percent of Yemeni children between the ages of six and fifteen to attend school. Instead, these children are forced by their parents to work on the streets or in the agricultural fields to earn money for the family's survival. Without an education, there is little hope that a child living in such poverty will ever experience anything but the same.

In many cases children are given by their own parents to traffickers who then take them across the border to Saudi Arabia, where it is fairly easy for cheap labor to be employed on the streets. At the hands of the wrong people, these children are exploited and abused, often repeatedly. It's hard to determine the greater villain; a parent who would sell his child for the sake of family income, or a person who makes a living off the misfortunes of others and preys on the most vulnerable of society. Either way, it is the children who suffer the greatest consequences. Tens of thousands of Yemeni children are smuggled annually to Saudi Arabia as beggars and servants. In 2006, only three children were reported missing by their own parents. The idea of families living off the earnings of their banished children is disturbing, yet in this impoverished country it is a common by-product of a decayed economic system. In fact, it is the deportation of their children from Saudi Arabia that some parents fear most, not their child's safety. The Ministry of Social Affairs acknowledged that as many as three hundred Yemeni children are caught in Saudi Arabia each month. What happens after they're caught only deepens the tragedy. Held at border crossing confinement camps along with adult deportees, the children are subject to further abuse. The most tragic cases are the very young; the five- and six-year-olds that are not old enough to tell authorities where they're from and are therefore sentenced to an extended stay in detention.

In whatever situation the children find themselves, laboring on the streets of Yemen, in the agricultural fields exposed to dangerous chemicals, or at the hands of criminals trafficking them to Saudi Arabia, they are being abused and denied an education. The solution needs to address the root of the problem which is poverty. Parents who genuinely want to do right, should be helped so that they have economic options, while those who abuse their parental rights, should be punished. In all cases, parents need to be educated on the importance of keeping their children in school. The concept that poverty begets child labor, and child labor begets poverty needs to be driven home until education automatically becomes the backdrop to every child's life.

Did you know... Yemen is one of the most under developed countries in the world with over eight and a half million people living below the poverty line?

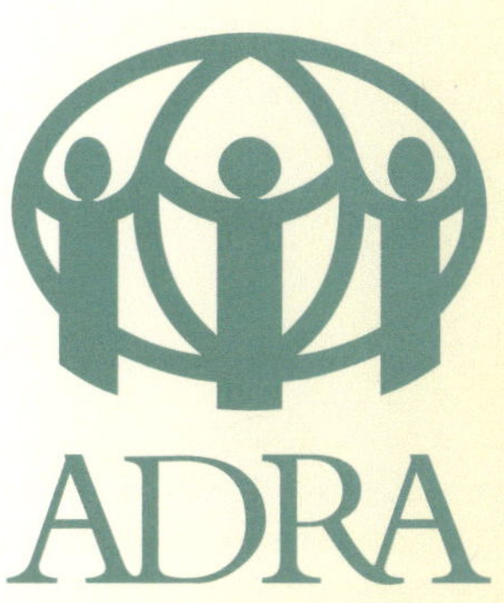

Adventist Development and Relief Agency

The Adventist Development and Relief Agency (ADRA) is a global humanitarian organization established by the Seventh-day Adventist Church. With a presence in more than 120 countries, ADRA demonstrates God's love and compassion by providing individual and community development and emergency relief assistance to those affected by natural or humanitarian disasters.

ADRA operates on the front lines of the most vulnerable societies in our world, restoring hope to those whose reality is poverty, hunger, disease, and illiteracy—partnering with individuals, communities, organizations, and governments to improve the quality of life for millions.

ADRA seeks to identify and address social injustice and deprivation in developing countries. The agency's work seeks to improve the quality of life of those in need and invests in the potential of these individuals through community development initiatives targeting through five main focus areas: Food Security and Availability; Economic Development; Primary Health, Water and Sanitation; Education; and Emergency Management.

Help ADRA Help Others

www.adra.org

Each year, ADRA brings lasting, positive change to more than 25 million people. In 2006, ADRA helped more than 26 million people with assistance valued at more than $145 million.

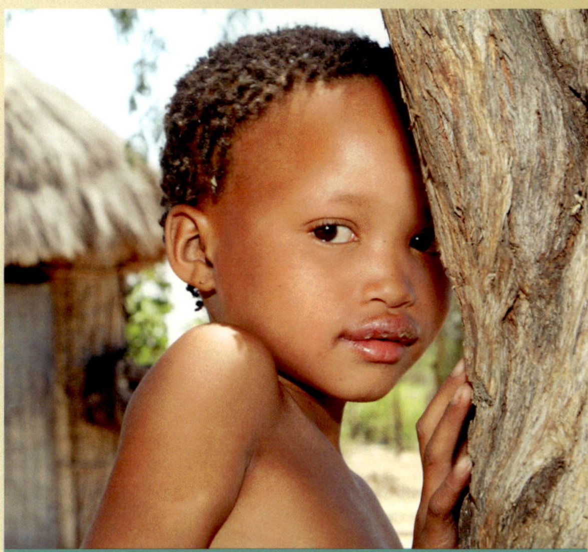

ADRA serves people without regard to their race or ethnicity, political affiliation, gender, or religious association. It simply helps people in need, especially the most vulnerable, such as women, children, and the elderly.

ADRA Yemen

Since 1995, ADRA has been helping the Yemeni people to overcome poverty, disease, and illiteracy through supporting local potential in solving problems and creating sustainable, productive solutions. Based on the local needs of the people, ADRA's programs enable communities to use their skills for long-term economic development and to develop local ownership of resources and facilities.

ADRA's activities in Yemen focus on primary health, economic development, education, and food security and availability. Projects focus on helping women, children, those living in poverty, as well as refugees and people with special needs.

Caring for Children

In an ongoing project, ADRA Yemen is changing the lives of those who face physical challenges, with a special focus on children. ADRA staff members provide physical therapy to persons with disabilities; refer patients for medical exams and assistive devices such as wheelchairs and limb prosthetics for landmine survivors; train caregivers to give patients in-home therapy; and lecture on health issues in the communities.

A major component of the project identifies and refers children with cleft lips or cleft palates for life-changing corrective surgery. With their smiles restored and their faces brightened with hope, the children look forward to a promising future.

Several of ADRA Yemen's programs that focus on providing humanitarian aid—including vocational skills and business training, local integration, and conflict mitigation—to the thousands of Somali refugees living in south Yemen, also focus on children.

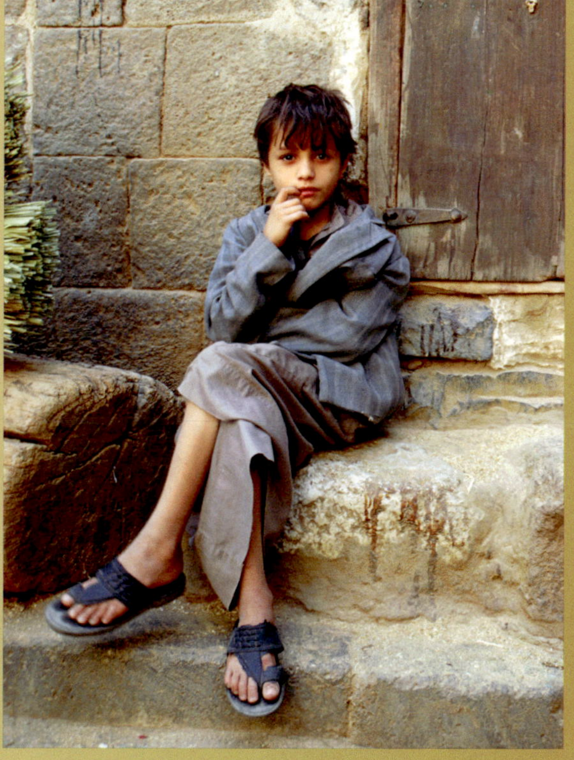

ADRA International Headquarters • 12501 Old Columbia Pike • Silver Spring, MD 20904 • www.adra.org • 800-424-2372

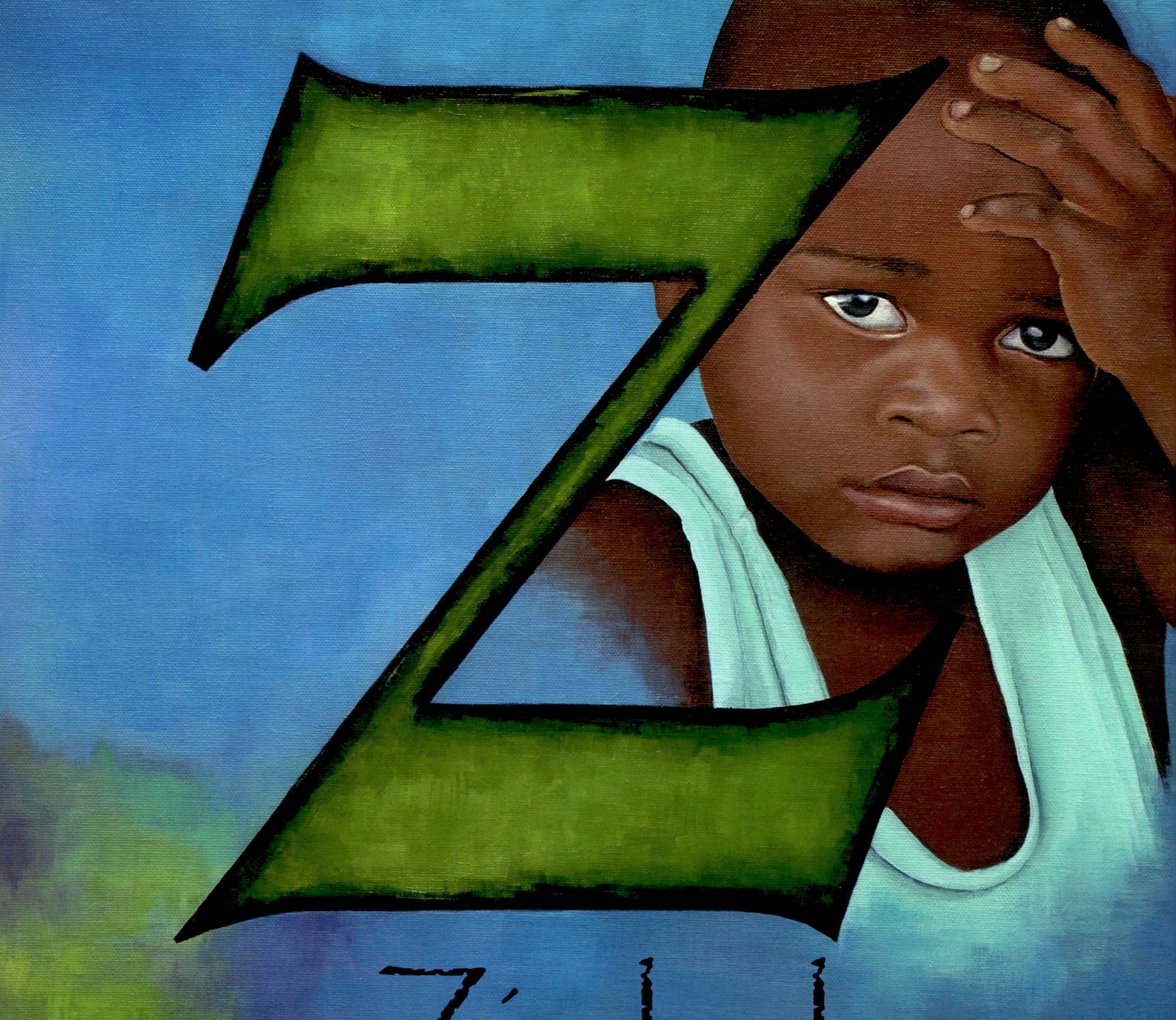

Z is for Zimbabwe

Yesterday

Today it's just the two of us
No father and no mother.
She is just a little girl
Left to raise a little brother.

Our parents died from AIDS.
It's very common here.
It's the children left behind
With the most to fear.

All alone, what should we do?
I don't even know.
I'm scared. I'm sad.
I wish I knew,
Why they had to go.

Before she died, mama said,
"Look after your baby brother."
Yesterday, she was my sister.
Today, she is my mother.

" When evil men plot, good men must plan. When evil men burn and bomb, good men must build and bind. When evil men shout ugly words of hatred, good men must commit themselves to the glories of love. Where evil men would seek to perpetuate an unjust status quo, good men must seek to bring into being a real order of justice"

–Martin Luther King, Jr.

About "Yesterday"

ON APRIL 18, 1980, a country in southern Africa gained its independence, a new flag was raised, a new government was born, and a new leader named. That country was Zimbabwe. Today the country is facing a catastrophic humanitarian crisis. Atrocities are being committed by the president and his ruthless regime. From corruption, violence and the systematic destruction of the economy to the devastation of AIDS, Zimbabweans have seen it all. The rest of the world should be outraged by the crimes that have been committed in this country.

During the Zanu PF regime, many of the government's ill intents have been exposed. Zimbabwe's current president, Robert Mugabe, was quoted as saying, "Absolute power is when man is starving and you are the only one able to give him food." As the story unfolds, that absolute power has become meaningless. There is no food to give, a twist of irony for those of us half a world away as we watch the undoing of a tyrant by his own hand. His misuse of his country's resources and lack of concern for the welfare of his people have led to the ongoing nightmare that is Zimbabwe today.

No part of Zimbabwean society has been more abused by its present government than the children. The education system has disintegrated to such an extent that there is little, if any, hope of a stable economic future. The health system is utterly failing and children are dying unnecessarily. Food shortages are rampant and show no signs of improvement. AIDS is devastating Zimbabwe's families. It is estimated that a quarter of the population is infected with the HIV virus. In Zimbabwe, the chances of a child either being left behind as an orphan or being infected with AIDS is greater than any other prospect awaiting them.

The children of Zimbabwe are facing incredible odds. The country's economic condition has become life-threatening to all but the ruling elite. With the inflation rate out of control at over one hundred thousand percent, Zimbabwe currency is worthless. As a result, basic products like sugar, cooking oil, flour and meat are typically only available on the black market. The unemployment rate has soared to over eighty percent causing a mass migration from the country. Three out of four Zimbabweans with jobs work outside of the country's borders. Those who emigrate for work often leave behind families and never come back. Sadly, children left behind to care for younger siblings are a common by-product of this exodus. Even sadder are the children orphaned by AIDS, forgotten by a country in crisis and therefore forced to make this exodus themselves, a trek that puts them in extreme danger, targets of gangs and traffickers.

When a government is motivated by ultimate power and greed, without a shred of regard for its people, we should all be gravely concerned. When a government mismanages its land, thus denying its people the ability to earn a living and ultimately creates a climate of mass unemployment and starvation, we should all be gravely concerned. When a government reacts with violence to any opposition and shows absolutely no sign of redemption, we should all be gravely concerned. When a government turns its back on its children, literally leaving them alone to fend for themselves, vulnerable and afraid, we should all be more than concerned. We should be outraged.

Far, far away, little voices need to be heard…Who is listening? The people of Zimbabwe are suffering, but it is the voices of children, if we listen to them, that will tell us fully of their heartbreak.

Did you know… It is estimated that one out of every eight adults in Zimbabwe has HIV?

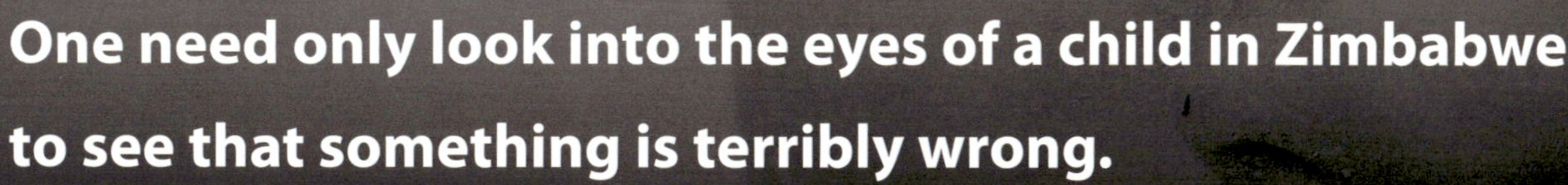

This page does not have the participation of an NGO in light of the current political situation in Zimbabwe. I chose not to jeopardize the incredible work different organizations are doing on the ground by asking them to stand by the words I have written about the current government. I believe with absolute conviction that when governments in our world are so riddled with corruption that people become uncomfortable with speaking the truth; the truth becomes even more important. I am not in Zimbabwe and I am blessed to have freedoms that the people there may never experience. These freedoms are exactly why I took this stance.

I cannot conclude this book or leave the issue of the innocent children of Zimbabwe without saying this: At some point, we must say enough…no more corruption, no more self serving politics and tyrannical leaders, no more abuses and no more impunity given through our tolerance and silence. Too many people suffer in the shadows of the world's dictators. The children of Zimbabwe need our help, to fight AIDS, to overcome poverty and to realize their deserved human rights. The children of the world need our attention, our compassion and our refusal to give up on them in spite of the governments they live under.

Please learn more about Zimbabwe and the suffering of her people. Visit the following web sites and find out how you can help ease their pain.

HIV/AIDS Zimbabwe (HAZ) - www.hivaidszimbabwe.org

International Development Exchange (IDEX) - www.idex.org

Doctors Without Borders - www.doctorswithoutborders.org

"One hundred years from now, it will not matter what my bank account was, how big my house was, or what kind of car I drove. But the world may be a little better, because I was important in the life of a child."

–Forest Witcraft, American Scholar and Teacher

Universal Declaration of Human Rights

On December 10, 1948 the General Assembly of the United Nations adopted and proclaimed the Universal Declaration of Human Rights the full text of which appears in the following pages. Following this historic act the Assembly called upon all Member countries to publicize the text of the Declaration and "to cause it to be disseminated, displayed, read and expounded principally in schools and other educational institutions, without distinction based on the political status of countries or territories."

Article 1.

All human beings are born free and equal in dignity and rights. They are endowed with reason and conscience and should act towards one another in a spirit of brotherhood.

Article 2.

Everyone is entitled to all the rights and freedoms set forth in this Declaration, without distinction of any kind, such as race, colour, sex, language, religion, political or other opinion, national or social origin, property, birth or other status. Furthermore, no distinction shall be made on the basis of the political, jurisdictional or international status of the country or territory to which a person belongs, whether it be independent, trust, non-self-governing or under any other limitation of sovereignty.

Article 3.

Everyone has the right to life, liberty and security of person.

Article 4.

No one shall be held in slavery or servitude; slavery and the slave trade shall be prohibited in all their forms.

Article 5.

No one shall be subjected to torture or to cruel, inhuman or degrading treatment or punishment.

Article 6.

Everyone has the right to recognition everywhere as a person before the law.

Article 7.

All are equal before the law and are entitled without any discrimination to equal protection of the law. All are entitled to equal protection against any discrimination in violation of this Declaration and against any incitement to such discrimination.

Article 8.

Everyone has the right to an effective remedy by the competent national tribunals for acts violating the fundamental rights granted him by the constitution or by law.

Article 9.

No one shall be subjected to arbitrary arrest, detention or exile.

Article 10.

Everyone is entitled in full equality to a fair and public hearing by an independent and impartial tribunal, in the determination of his rights and obligations and of any criminal charge against him.

Article 11.

1. Everyone charged with a penal offence has the right to be presumed innocent until proved guilty according to law in a public trial at which he has had all the guarantees necessary for his defence.
2. No one shall be held guilty of any penal offence on account of any act or omission which did not constitute a penal offence, under national or international law, at the time when it was committed. Nor shall a heavier penalty be imposed than the one that was applicable at the time the penal offence was committed.

Article 12.

No one shall be subjected to arbitrary interference with his privacy, family, home or correspondence, nor to attacks upon his honour and reputation. Everyone has the right to the protection of the law against such interference or attacks.

Article 13.

1. Everyone has the right to freedom of movement and residence within the borders of each state.
2. Everyone has the right to leave any country, including his own, and to return to his country.

Article 14.

1. Everyone has the right to seek and to enjoy in other countries asylum from persecution.
2. This right may not be invoked in the case of prosecutions genuinely arising from non-political crimes or from acts contrary to the purposes and principles of the United Nations.

Article 15.

1. Everyone has the right to a nationality.
2. No one shall be arbitrarily deprived of his nationality nor denied the right to change his nationality.

Article 16.

1. Men and women of full age, without any limitation due to race, nationality or religion, have the right to marry and to found a family. They are entitled to equal rights as to marriage, during marriage and at its dissolution.
2. Marriage shall be entered into only with the free and full consent of the intending spouses.
3. The family is the natural and fundamental group unit of society and is entitled to protection by society and the State.

Article 17.

1. Everyone has the right to own property alone as well as in association with others.
2. No one shall be arbitrarily deprived of his property.

Article 18.

Everyone has the right to freedom of thought, conscience and religion; this right includes freedom to change his religion or belief, and freedom, either alone or in community with others and in public or private, to manifest his religion or belief in teaching, practice, worship and observance.

Article 19.

Everyone has the right to freedom of opinion and expression; this right includes freedom to hold opinions without interference and to seek, receive and impart information and ideas through any media and regardless of frontiers.

Article 20.

1. Everyone has the right to freedom of peaceful assembly and association.
2. No one may be compelled to belong to an association.

Article 21.

1. Everyone has the right to take part in the government of his country, directly or through freely chosen representatives.
2. Everyone has the right of equal access to public service in his country.
3. The will of the people shall be the basis of the authority of government; this will shall be expressed in periodic and genuine elections which shall be by universal and equal suffrage and shall be held by secret vote or by equivalent free voting procedures.

Article 22.

Everyone, as a member of society, has the right to social security and is entitled to realization, through national effort and international co-operation and in accordance with the organization and resources of each State, of the economic, social and cultural rights indispensable for his dignity and the free development of his personality.

Article 23.

1. Everyone has the right to work, to free choice of employment, to just and favourable conditions of work and to protection against unemployment.
2. Everyone, without any discrimination, has the right to equal pay for equal work.
3. Everyone who works has the right to just and favourable remuneration ensuring for himself and his family an existence worthy of human dignity, and supplemented, if necessary, by other means of social protection.
4. Everyone has the right to form and to join trade unions for the protection of his interests.

Article 24.

Everyone has the right to rest and leisure, including reasonable limitation of working hours and periodic holidays with pay.

Article 25.

1. Everyone has the right to a standard of living adequate for the health and well-being of himself and of his family, including food, clothing, housing and medical care and necessary social services, and the right to security in the event of unemployment, sickness, disability, widowhood, old age or other lack of livelihood in circumstances beyond his control.
2. Motherhood and childhood are entitled to special care and assistance. All children, whether born in or out of wedlock, shall enjoy the same social protection.

Article 26.

1. Everyone has the right to education. Education shall be free, at least in the elementary and fundamental stages. Elementary education shall be compulsory. Technical and professional education shall be made generally available and higher education shall be equally accessible to all on the basis of merit.
2. Education shall be directed to the full development of the human personality and to the strengthening of respect for human rights and fundamental freedoms. It shall promote understanding, tolerance and friendship among all nations, racial or religious groups, and shall further the activities of the United Nations for the maintenance of peace.
3. Parents have a prior right to choose the kind of education that shall be given to their children.

Article 27.

1. Everyone has the right freely to participate in the cultural life of the community, to enjoy the arts and to share in scientific advancement and its benefits.
2. Everyone has the right to the protection of the moral and material interests resulting from any scientific, literary or artistic production of which he is the author.

Article 28.

Everyone is entitled to a social and international order in which the rights and freedoms set forth in this Declaration can be fully realized.

"Children are the living messages we send to a time we will not see."
–John W. Whitehead, Founder-Rutherford Institute

Article 29.

1. Everyone has duties to the community in which alone the free and full development of his personality is possible.
2. In the exercise of his rights and freedoms, everyone shall be subject only to such limitations as are determined by law solely for the purpose of securing due recognition and respect for the rights and freedoms of others and of meeting the just requirements of morality, public order and the general welfare in a democratic society.
3. These rights and freedoms may in no case be exercised contrary to the purposes and principles of the United Nations.

Article 30.

Nothing in this Declaration may be interpreted as implying for any State, group or person any right to engage in any activity or to perform any act aimed at the destruction of any of the rights and freedoms set forth herein.

Photo Credits

A is for Afghanistan

Artwork–Photo referenced (with permission) was taken by **Luke Powell,** titled **"Smiling Girl"** (Location–Rohani Refugee Camp in Chaman, Pakistan, November 2001). Luke lives in Liverpool, Nova Scotia Canada and is a professional photographer. **www.lukepowell.com**

Women for Women page–"3 Generations" & **"Women with Blue Burkas",** both photos courtesy of **Women for Women International.**

B is for Bangladesh

Artwork–Photo referenced (with permission) was taken by **Greg Miles,** titled **"Bangla Village Girl"** (Location–a rural village in Bangladesh). Greg lives in Australia and is a Nurseryman and Volunteer Photographer.

The Hunger Project page–Photo courtesy of **The Hunger Project,** (Location Bangladesh).

C is for Cambodia

Artwork–Photo referenced (with permission) was taken by **Sam Tan,** titled **"Praying Children"** (Location–Kampung Chiam, Cambodia). Sam lives in Puchong, Malaysia. **www.flickr.com/photos/myshoebox, thedigitalshoebox.samuel@gmail.com**

Cambodian Children's Fund page–Photo courtesy of **Cambodian Children's Fund.**

D is for Djibouti

Artwork–Photo referenced (with permission) was taken by **Guuleed A. Hussein,** titled **"Two Girls"** (Location–Djibouti). Guuleed, a Somalia immigrant residing in Canada, is a Photo Journalist/Editor Pace Magazine/ Founder of Guproductions.

Project C.U.R.E. page– "Hospital Reality", photo courtesy of **Jason M. Corley** (Location–Lagos General Hospital, Nigeria). Jason lives in Arizona USA, and is the Director of Global Outreach for the Central Church of East Valley in Arizona.

E is for Ethiopia

Artwork–Photo referenced (with permission) was taken by **Frans Devriese,** titled **"Arbore tribe #5"** (Location–Extreme Southwest Ethiopia). Frans lives in Belgium and is a Clinical Laboratory Assistant (bacteriology)/ Motivated Traveler.

Action Against Hunger page–"Big eyes", photo courtesy of **Burger/Phanie,** (Location–Congo). **"Plates",** photo courtesy of **M.Attwood/Agence VU,** (Location–Malawi).

F is for Fiji

Artwork–Photo referenced (with permission) was taken by **Alex Kehr,** titled **"Lion Boy"** (Location–Raki Raki Village, Fiji, taken while doing Community Service with Global Works Inc.). Alex lives in Malibu, CA USA and is a Student.

Shared Hope International page–"Linda with Children from the Home of Hope in Fiji, October 2005", photo courtesy of **Shared Hope International.**

G is for Guatemala

Artwork–Photo referenced (with permission) was taken by **Cammy Challender,** titled **"Beautiful Guatamalan Children"** (Location–San Marcos La Laguna on Lake Atitlan, Guatemala). Cammy lives in Lawrence, Kansas and is a Case Manager for Big Brothers, Big Sisters.

Friendship Bridge page–"M. Santos, Llanos de Pinal, Quetzaltenango, Guatemala" & **"M. Luisa's Daughter & Son, Poxlajuj, Totonicapán, Guatemala",** both photos courtesy of **Nancy Lewis & Randy Fay. www.hobobiker.com**

H is for Haiti

Artwork–Photo referenced (with permission) was taken by **Tom Woltjer,** titled **"108543179-L"** (Location–Don Bosco, Dominican Republic, taken on a mission with Children of the Nations–**www.cotni.org**). Tom lives in Port Orchard, WA USA and is a Photographer. **www.tomsimages.com**

Beyond Borders page– "Reunion", photo courtesy of **Tom Woltjer** (Location–Don Bosco, Dominican Repulic). **"Cabbage Farm Kids",** photo courtesy of **Marcia Willson** (Location–Gros Cheval, Haiti).

I is for Indonesia

Artwork–Photo referenced (with permission) was taken by **Franc Le Blanc,** titled **"Timor N.T.T. desa Tuapukan . Camp pengungsian"** (Location–Timor Leste, near Dili, Indonesia). Franc lives in the Netherlands and is an Artist/Photographer. **www.yamdena.tk**

World Neighbors page–Photo courtesy of **Brandon Hoover,** (Location–Jakarta Indonesia). Brandon is a Photographer/ Teacher. **www.javajive.com**

J is for Jamaica

Artwork–Photo referenced (with permission) was taken by **Sue Steege,** titled **"Claudine"** (Location–Children of Israel Orphanage, Les Cayes, Haiti). Sue lives in Tonawanda, NY USA and is the Director of Transportation Ministries.

Photo Credits cont.

SOS Children's Villages-USA page– Photo courtesy of **SOS Children's Villages-USA.**

K is for Kenya

Artwork–Photo referenced (with permission) was taken by **Graham Wallen,** titled **"Kenyan Children"** (Location–Turtle Bay Beach, Watamu, Kenya). Graham lives in Laverstock, Salisbury Wiltshire UK and is a Taxi Driver.

Blood:Water Mission page–Photos courtesy of **Blood:Water Mission.**

L is for Lebanon

Artwork–Photo referenced (with permission) was taken by **Jim Gordon,** titled **"Iraqi girl at medical screening"** (Location–Habiniyah, Iraq) Jim lives in Biloxi, MS USA and is a US Government Photographer.

Mercy Corps page–Photos courtesy of **Casandra Nelson/Mercy Corps** (Location–Lebanon).

M is for Myanmar

Artwork–Photo referenced (with permission) courtesy of **www.asianinsights.org,** titled **"Child carrying child"** (Location–Nagaland, Burma)

US Campaign for Burma page–"child" & "mother and children", both photos courstesy of **Free Burma Rangers. "Monks"** courtesy of **US Campaign for Burma** (Public Domain).

N is for Nepal

Artwork–Photo referenced (with permission) was taken by **Gunnar Geir Pétursso,** titled **"Nepali Child"** (Location–Langtang National Park bordering in north-northeast Nepal). Gunnar lives in Iceland and is a Photographer.

NYOF page–"Children of the Mountains" courtesy of **Mitchell Kanashkevich**. Mitchell lives in Austrailia. **"Three Nepali Children"** courtesy of **David Allen and Aid for Nepali Children wwwaidfornepalichildren.org.uk** (Location–the Dolakha region of northeast Nepal)

O is for Oman

Artwork–Photo referenced (with permission) was taken by **Phil Wingfield,** titled **"Ardh Mela Girl"** (Location–Ardh Kundh Mela, Allahabad, India)

National Labor Committee page–"Young Labor", photo courtesy of **Eve Lyman** (Location–Afghanistan). Eve lives in Cambridge, MA USA and is a Photographer/Graphic Designer. **www.TheEyeoftheBeholder.net**

P is for Pakistan

Artwork–Photo referenced (with permission) was taken by **Nadir Burney,** titled **"Aysha"** (Location–Sindh, Pakistan).

Equality Now page–"Amazing Children", photo courtesy of **Kurt Langland** (Location–Rawalpindi, Pakistan). Kurt lives in Spokane, Washington, USA and is a Minister.

Q is for Qatar

Artwork–Photo referenced (with permission) was taken by **Abdulqadir,** titled **"Camel Jockey"** (Location–Qatar).

Global March page– Photo courtesy of **Global March Against Child Labour**

R is for Rwanda

Artwork–Photo referenced (with permission) was taken by **Kresta King Cutcher Venning**, titled **"Gisimba Memorial Center"** (Location– Gisimba Memorial Center, Nyamirambo, Kigali, Rwanda). Kresta King lives in MA, Bornemouth, UK and is a former Educator/ Photographer with Purpose. **www.sistersofrwanda.org www.orphansofrwanda.org**

Face AIDS page–Photos courtesy of **Katie Bolbach** (Location–Kirehe district of Rwanda). Katie lives in Rwanda and is Face AIDS co-founder and Africa Program Director.

S is for Sudan

Artwork–Photo referenced (with permission) was taken by **Caesar A, Ricci III,** titled **"Little Pink Dress"** (Location–Al –Talata ,Eastern Chad). Ceasar lives in San Antonio, TX, USA and is a Medical Student at UTHSCSA. **www.thegreatestgood.net**

ENOUGH Project page–"John & Child", photo courtesy of **Sally Chin/Enough Project**

T is for Tibet

Artwork–Photos referenced (with permission)- Beggar girl photo courtesy of **www.asianinsights.org www.asianisights.net,** titled **"derdscheladen – my sweet, little beggar friend"** (Location– Lhasa, Tibet). Monk boy photo courtesy of **Evren Savrin,** titled **"Tibetans/6"** (Location–Katmandu, Nepal). Evren lives in New Delhi, India (Originally Ankara, Turkey) and is a Photographer.

International Campaign for Tibet page-"Dalai Lama 08", photo courtesy of **Peter Heacox** (Location– Denver University,

Photo Credits cont.

Denver Peace Jam , Sept 2006). Peter lives in Evans, Colorado USA and is a Professional Photographer. **www.heacoxphotography.com** **"Children on Hill"**, photo courtesy of **Sonam Zoksang /International Campaign for Tibet.**

U is for Uganda

Artwork–Photo referenced (with permission) was taken by **Daina Goodwin,** titled **"IMG_5162.jpg"** (Location–Gulu, Uganda).

Invisible Children page–"Filmmakers Bobby Bailey, Laren Poole and Jason Russell in northern Uganda" & "Child mother in northern Uganda", both photos courtesy of **Invisible Children, Inc.**

V is for Vietnam

Artwork–Photo referenced (with permission) was taken by **Andreas Weinert,** titled **"Innocence by A. Weinert"** (Location–Mekong Delta, Vietnam). Andreas lives in Sydney, Australia.

East Meets West page–"Student in Central Vietnam", photo courtesy of **Tom Low.**

W is for Western Sahara

Artwork–Photo referenced (with permission) was taken by **Extrujadu,** titled **"Saharan girl/nina saharaui"** (Location–refugee camp Tindouf, Algeria). Extrujadu lives in Spain and is a teacher.

War On Want page–"Pequeños de Smara", photo courtesy of **Álvaro Herraiz San Martin** (Location– refugee camp Algeria). Álvaro lives in Madrid, Castilla Spain and is a student. **"Sahauri Children"**, photo courtesy of **War on Want.**

X is for Xanadu

Americans for Informed Democracy page–"Globe in Hands", photo courtesy of **Americans for Informed Democracy.**

Y is for Yemen

Artwork–Photo referenced (with permission) was taken by **Walter Callens,** titled **"Yemen"** (Location–Northern Yemen). Walter lives in Belgium and is a Photographer.

ADRA International page–Photos courtesy of **ADRA International.**

Z is for Zimbabwe

Artwork–Photo referenced (with permission) was taken by **Justin Nash,** titled **"Zimbabwe 1019"** (Location–Zimbabwe). Justin lives in Amarillo, Texas USA.

Zimbabwe statement page–"Reflection – Deeply Responsive to the World", photo courtesy of **Hannah Galli (Inneri)**, (Location–Salt Lake City). Hannah lives in Salt Lake City, Utah USA and is a Graphic Designer, Freelance Photographer, and Vocalist. **www.partners.utah.edu/programs/hartlandapartments.htm**

The Declaration of Human Rights

"Kenyan Children" (page 117), photo courtesy of **Graham Wallen** (Location– Turtle Bay Beach, Watamu, Kenya). Graham lives in Laverstock, Salisbury Wiltshire UK and is a Taxi Driver.

"Beautiful Guatamalan Children" (page 118), photo courtesy of **Cammy Challender** (Location–San Marcos La Laguna on Lake Atitlan, Guatemala). Cammy lives in Lawrence, Kansas USA and is a Case Manager/Big Brothers, Big Sisters.

"Indonesian Children crw6976" (page 119), photo courtesy of **Brandon Hoover.** Brandon lives in Jakarta, Indonesia and is a Photographer/Teacher. **www.thejavajive.com**

References

A is for Afghanistan

- Coursen-Neff, Zama, Senior Researcher, Children's Rights Division "The Taliban's War on Education: Schoolgirls are still under fire in Afghanistan." LA Times. July. 2006. 28 Mar.2007 <http://www.hrw.org/english/docs/2006/08/21/afghan14057_txt.htm>.
- "Humanitarian Action Report 2007 ROSA Afghanistan." UNICEF. 26 Dec. 2007 <http://www.unicef.org/har07/index_37575.htm>.
- "UNICEF appeals for more aid to help women, children." IRIN. July 2007. 26 Dec. 2007 <http://www.irinnews.org/PrintReport.aspx?ReportId=73444>.
- "UNICEF report says time is running out on Afghanistan children, Progress in health and education endangered by recent surges in violence." UNICEF. Oct. 2007. 26 Dec. 2007 <http://www.unicef.org/media/media_41387.html>.

B is for Bangladesh

- "Children in Poor Countries Need Help." World Population Awareness–Children Report. Nov. 2006. 13 Mar. 2007 <http://www.overpopulation.org/children.html>.
- Professor Majumdar, Badiul Alam. "Protect the Girl Child for a prosperous Bangladesh." The Hunger Project. Sept. 2002. 26 Nov. 2007 <http://www.thp.org/bangladesh/dailystar/index.html>.
- Stoparic, Bojan. "Anti-Poverty Efforts Face Child Marriage Hurdle." WomensEnews. Sept. 2006. 13 Mar.2007<http://www.womensenews.org/article.cfm/dyn/aid/2831/context/archive>.
- Thakur, Ramesh & Ahmed, Manzoor. "Children in Poor Nations Still Need Help." International Herald Tribune. Dec. 1999. <http://www.iht.com/articles/1999/12/30/edram.t.php>.
- Wax, Emily. "Bangladeshi child star highlights plight of girls. "Washington Post. Sept. 2007.25 Nov. 2007 <http://www.boston.com/news/world/asia/articles/2007/09/16/bangladeshi_child_star_highlights_plight_of_girls/>.

C is for Cambodia

- "Essential Background: Overview of human rights issues in Cambodia." Human Rights Watch, World Report. 2007. 6 May 2007 <http://hrw.org/englishwr2k7/docs/2007/01/11/cambod14866.htm>.
- Hayes, Michael. "Aging Khmer Rouge living in denial." Phnom Penh Post. Apr. 2000 <http://www.phnompenhpost.com/TXT/comments/aging.htm>.
- "Pol Pot killer file-moreorless: heroes & killers of the 20th century." More or Less. 6 May. 2007 <http://www.moreorless.au.com/killers/pot.html>.
- "Pol Pot: Life of a tyrant." BBC News. Apr. 2000. 6 May 2007 <http://news.bbc.co.uk/1/hi/world/asia-pacific/78988.stm>.

D is for Djibouti

- "Djibouti Facts and Figures." CERF around the world. May 2007. 26 Jan. 2008 <http://ochaonline.un.org/default.aspx>.
- "Djibouti Food Security Update January 2008–Pastoral Food Access decreases as season fails." Famine Early Warning System Network. Jan. 2008. 26 Jan. 2008 <http://www.reliefweb.int/rw/RWB.NSF/db900SID/ASIN-7B4MDZ?OpenDocument>.
- "Djibouti: Malnutrition widespread in drought-affected areas." IRIN Humanitarian News and Analysis. June 2005. 1 Mar. 2008 <http://www.irinnews.org/report.aspx?reportid=54777>.
- "MENA Djibouti: Emergency Summary." Humanitarian Action Report. 1 Mar. 2008 <http://www.unicef.org/har08/index_djibouti.php>.
- "WFP plans to stop feeding 53,000 people in Djibouti as funds run out." World Food Programme. Mar. 2007. 27 Dec. 2007 <http://www.wfp.org/english/?ModuleID=137&Key=2419>.

E is for Ethiopia

- "Ethiopia: Nearly half of the children orphaned by HIV/AIDS." IRIN Humanitarian News Analysis. Oct. 2005. 26 Jan. 2008 <http://www.irinnews.org/report.aspx?reportid=56823>.
- "Ethiopia: UN warns of humanitarian crisis in Somali Region." IRIN Humanitarian News and Analysis. UN Office. Oct. 2007. 4 Nov. 2007 <http://www.irinnews.org/report.aspx?Reportid=74666>.
- "Horn of Africa: The pastoralists way of life-a fragile future for millions of children." IRIN Humanitarian News and Analysis. UN Office. Oct. 2007. 4 Nov. 2007 <http://www.irinnews.org/report.aspx?Reportid=75051>.
- Kristof, Nicholas D. "Ethiopia's Dying Children." New York Times Company. May 2003. 5 Jan. 2008 <http://query.nytimes.com/gst/fullpage.html>.
- "UN: Atrocities Fuel Worsening Crisis in Horn of Africa." Dec. 2007. 17 Jan. 2008 <http://hrw.org/english/docs/2007/11/30/somali17457_txt.htm>.
- Zarifi, Sam. "Human Rights Watch Testimony at hearing of the house committee on foreign affairs subcommittee on Africa and Global Health." Human Rights Watch. Oct. 2007. 7 Jan. 2008 <http://www.hrw.org/english/docs/2007/10/03/ethiop17010_txt.htm>.

F is for Fiji

- Ali, Shamima. "Violence against the girl child in the Pacific Islands region." United Nations Division for the Advancement with Women (DAW) in collaboration with UNICEF. EGM/DVGC/2006?EP.14
- "Fiji Background" UNICEF. 10 Apr. 2008 <http://www.unicef.org/infobycountry/fiji.html?q=printme>.

- “New report exposes the problem and nature of sexual violence against children in five Pacific countries.” UNICEF EAPRO. Dec 2006. 10 Apr. 2008. <http://www.unicef.org/eapro/media_5439.html>.
- “Shekhar: Stop the violence against children.” Fiji Times Online. Mar. 2008. 10 Apr. 2008. <http://www.fijitimes.com/story.aspx?id=83997>.

G is for Guatemala

- “Canadian documentary focuses on plight of Guatemalan women.” CBC Arts. Mar. 2007. 13 Mar. 2007 <http://www.cbc.ca/arts/film/story/2007/03/08/guatemala-women.html>.
- “Guatemala Human Rights Update.” Guatemala Human Rights Commission/USA. Jan. 2008. <http://www.ghrc-usa.org>.
- “Mexico and Guatemala: Stop the killings of Women.” Amnesty International USA. Jan. 2007. 5 Mar. 2007 <http://www.amnestyusa.org/document.php?lang=e&id=ENGUSA20070130001>.
- Rosenberg, Mica. “Violence Plagues Guatemala decade after war’s end.” ABC News International. Dec. 2006. 5 Mar. 2007 <http://abcnews.go.com/International/wireStory.id=2754630>.
- “Stop the Killings of women in Guatemala.” Stop Violence Against Women. 5 Mar. 2007. <http://www.amnestyusa.org/women/guatemala/>.

H is for Haiti

- “Executive Director visits UNICEF-supported projects on first official visit to Haiti, Port-Au- Prince, Haiti.” UNICEF. Jan. 2008. 18 Jan. 2008 <http://www.unicef.org/infobycountry/haiti_42374.html>.
- Kavanagh, Michael J. “Dispatches From Haiti, The poor get poorer.” Slate. Sept. 2005. 18 Jan. 2008 <http://www.slate.com/toolbar.aspx?action=print&id=2125248>.
- Roig-Franzia, Manuel. “Imprisoned in Haiti at age 8.”The Washington Post. Nation & World. The Seattle Times. 5 Mar. 2007 <http://seattletimes.nwsource.com/html/nationworld/2003600005_haitikids04.html>.
- Russell, Carmen & Liu, Dane. “Kids forced into domestic servitude in Haiti.” MSNBC. Aug. 2007. 7 Jan. 2008 <http://www.msnbc.msn.com/id/20293963/>.

I is for Indonesia

- “Child Trafficking: An Awakening.” kNOw Child Labour. Feb. 2008. 3 Mar. 2008 <http://www.globalmarch.org/news/index.php>.
- “Child protection from violence, exploitation and abuse.” UNICEF. 3 Mar. 2008 <http://unicef.org/protection/index_childlabour.html>.
- “Indonesia: Save the Children.” Save the Children Web site. 4 Nov. 2007 <http://www.savethechildren.org/countries/asia/indonesia.html>.
- “Most People have no idea how large the problem is ‘RINA.” Child Exploitation. 10 Jan. 2008 <http://www.childexploitation.org/reallives7.html>.
- “Poverty ‘main cause’ of trafficking.” Jakarta Post. Poverty News Blog. Oct. 2007. 10 Jan. 2008 <http://www.povertynewsblog.blogspot.com/2007/10/poverty-main-cause-of-trafficking.html>.
- Vitiello, Christine. “Cocoa, Coffee, and Child Slave Labor.” IHS Child Slave Labor News. Nov. 2005. 3 Mar. 2008 <http://ihscslnews.org/view_article.php?id=43>.

J is for Jamaica

- “Jamaica: Infants face severe punishment, says violence expert.” (CRIN) Child’s Rights Information Network. Feb. 2008. 5 Mar. 2008 <http://www.crin.org/resources/infoDetail.asp?ID=16520&flag=report>.
- “Jamaicans Unite for Peace.” UNICEF Tacro . Feb. 2008. 5 Mar. 2008 <http://www.unicef.org/lac/english_11464.htm>.
- “Sun, Sea and Murder.” Economist Print Edition. Jan. 2008. 5 Mar. 2008 <http://www.economist.com/world/la/displaystory.cfm?story_id=10609414>.
- “The Conundrum of Violence in Jamaica.” Dec. 2007. <http://Livingbarbados.blogspot.com/2007/12/conundrum-of-violence-in-jamaica.html>.

K is for Kenya

- “AIDS Orphans.” Avert, Feb. 2008. 1 Mar. 2008 <http://www.avert.org/aidsorphans.htm>.
- “Africa: Letting Them Fail: Government Neglect and the right to Education for Children…Findings from Kenya South Africa, and Uganda.” Human Rights Watch. 17 Jan. 2008 <http://www.hrw.org/reports/2005/africa1005/4.htm>.
- “Kenyan Crisis: Continued Violence Challenges Service Delivery; Pathfinder Helps Ensure Needs Are Met.” Pathfinder International. Feb. 2008. 2 Mar. 2008 <http://www.pathfind.org/site/PageServer?pagename=Programs_Kenya_Crisis2008>.
- “Kenya: Political unrest sparks food insecurity, livelihood losses.” IRIN humanitarian news and analysis. Jan. 2008. 17 Jan. 2008 <http://www.irinnews.org/PrintReport.aspx?ReportId=76221>.
- Pollock, Abra. “Kenya: Violence Threatens Progress in HIV/AIDS Fight.” Interpress Service News Agency (IPS). Feb. 2008. 2 Mar. 2008 <http://ipsnews.net/print.asp?idnews=41123>.
- Svedberg, Linda.“Grand Parents Left with AIDS-Orphans; Challenges and Strategies Handling Poverty and Stigma.” Mid Sweden University.

L is for Lebanon

- Cook, Jonathan. "Evidence of Israel's 'cowardly blending' comes to light." Electronic Lebanon. An Electronic Intifada project found. Jan. 2008. 17 Jan. 2008 <http://electronicintifada.net/v2/article9200.shtml>.
- "Developments in Lebanon and Israel." Office of the special representative of the Secretary-General for Children and Armed Conflict. Oct. 2006. 27 Dec. 2007 <http://www.un.org/children/conflict/english/lebanonandisrael.html>.
- "Lebanon: Children traumatized by attacks." IRIN Humanitarian News & Analysis. UN Office for the Coordination of Humanitarian Affairs. July 2006. 17 Jan. 2008 <http://www.irinnews.org/report.aspx?reportid=59865>.

M is for Myanmar

- "Burma: Landmines Kill, Maim and Starve Civilians." Human Rights Watch. Dec. 2006. 27 Jan. 2008 <http://hrw.org/english/docs/2006/12/20/burma14904_txt.htm>.
- "Hollywood urges UN Chief to act for Myanmar's Suu Kyi." Stars for Burma, Celebrities supporting freedom and democracy in Burma. Sept. 2007. 7 Jan. 2008 <http://www.starsforburma.com/hollywood_burma.htm>.
- Mathieson, David Scott. "Child soldiers a problem in Myanmar." Human Rights Watch. Dec. 2007. 7 Jan. 2008 <http://hrw.org/english/docs/2007/12/05/burma17484_txt.htm>.
- Mathieson, David Scott. "Urgent action needed on rights in Burma." Human Rights Watch. The Nation. Oct. 2006. 7 Jan. 2008 <http://hrw.org/english/docs/2006/11/10/burma14553_txt.htm>.

N is for Nepal

- Bhattarai, Tara. "An Open Secret." The Press Institute for Women in the Developing World. Sept. 2007. 27 Dec. 2007 <http://piwdw.org/news/nepal/trafficked/index.html>.
- Haviland, Charles. "Desperate plight of Nepal 'slave girls." BBC News- Dang Western Nepal. Now Public crowd powered media. Mar. 2007. 27 Dec. 2007 <http://www.nowpublic.com/desperate_plight_of_nepal_slave_girls>.
- "High Rates of HIV infection Documented among young Nepalese Girls Sex-Trafficked to India." Harvard School of Public Health. July. 2007. 27 Dec. 2007 <http://www.hsph.harvard.edu/news/press-releases/2007-releases/press07312007.html>.
- Pradhan, Suman. "NEPAL: Selling Daughters into Bondage May End." Inter Press News Agency. Sept. 2006. 27 Dec. 2007 <http://www.ipsnews.net/print.asp?idnews=34755>.
- "The Day My God Died." Documentary Film on Sexual Trafficking in Nepal & India. 2003. Andrew Levine Productions USA: 70 Min.
- "Trafficking of Girls in Nepal." Refugee Watch Online. Feb. 2007. 27 Dec. 2007 <http://refugeewatchonline.blogspot.com/search>.
- "Trafficking of Nepali Girls." VOA News.com, Jan. 2007. 27 Dec. 2007 <www.voanews.com/uspolicy/archive/2007-01/2007-01-10-voa2.cfm>.

O is for Oman

- "Analysis of July 8 'Saturday Nights' Decree Issued by the Sultan of Oman." Democratic Staff of the House Ways and Means Committee. <http://www.citizen.org/documents/AnalysisJuly8SultanofOmanDecree.pdf>.
- "Freedom in the World–Oman 2007." Freedom House. 9 Jan. 2008 <http://www.freedomhouse.org/inc/content/pubs/fiw/inc_country_detail.cfm?year=2007&country=7246&pf>.
- Juhasz, Antonia."Trading on Terror to profit a few." MWC News. June. 2006. 9 Jan. 2008 <http://mwcnews.net/content/view/7869/26/>.
- "Most People have no idea how large the problem truly is…" Child Exploitation. 9 Jan. 2008 <http://www.childexploitation.org/labor36.html>.
- "On Jordan Standard and Bush's Corporate 'wink and a nod." Eyes on Trade. May 2007. 10 Jan. 2008 <http://citizen.typepad.com/eyesontrade/2007/05/sen_brown_on_jo.html>.
- "Remarks at the Release of 2007 Trafficking in Persons Report." Ambassador Mark. Lagon, Director, Office to Monitor and Combat Trafficking in Persons. Washington DC. June. 2007.
- Zunes, Stephen. "Congress Approves Flawed Oman Trade Pact." Silver City, NM and Washington, DC: Foreign Policy in Focus. July. 2006 <http://www.fpif.org/fpiftxt/3390>.

P is for Pakistan

- Arif, Malik Muhammad "Against Honor Killing and Domestic Violence." Ground Report. Mar 2008. 1 Apr. 2008. <http://www.groundreport.com/article.php?articleID=2856556&action=print_article>.
- "Pakistan: Haq Bakshish: No right to wed" IRIN - UN-OCHA Integrated Regional Information Networks. 8 Mar 2007 <http://www.irinnews.org/printReport.aspx?reportId=70564>.
- "Pakistan: Marriage by Exchange." IRIN - UN-OCHA Integrated Regional Information Networks. 8 Mar 2007 <http://www.irinnews.org/printReport.aspx?reportId=70577>.
- "Pakistan: Tribal custom forces girls into "compensation marriages" IRIN - UN-OCHA Integrated Regional Information Networks August 2003. 8 Mar. 2007. <http://www.irinnews.org/printReport.aspx?reportId=20618>.
- "Pakistan: Women pay to end family feuds" IRIN - UN-OCHA Integrated Regional Information Networks. 8 Mar. 2007. <http://www.irinnews.org/Report.aspx?ReportId=70573>.
- "Rights of the Child in Pakistan" World Organization Against Torture. Sep 2003. 8 Mar, 2007. <http://www.omct.org/pdf/cc/pakistan_report_09_2003_EN.pdf>.

Q is for Qatar

- "Pakistan: Focus on Rehabilitation of child jockeys." IRIN Humanitarian News and Analysis. 6 Dec. 2007 <http://www.irinnews.org/report.aspx?reportid=28689>.

- "Qatar Interior Ministry Promises to End Child Camel Jockey Slavery–A Good First Step." Human Rights News Forum. Church of Scientology International. July 2005. 5 Dec. 2007 <http://www.theta.com/human-trafficking/20050725_ht_1.php>.
- "Rescued child camel jockeys handed over to extremist groups" Ansar Burney Welfare Trust Sept. 2007. 6 Dec. 2007 <http://www.ansarburney.org/news/cj/cj49.html>.
- "Underage camel Jockeys in Saudi Arabia" Ansar Burney Welfare Trust. 6 Dec. 2007. <http://www.ansarburney.com/news1.htm#news2>.
- "UAE Commits $9 million to help former camel jockeys." Dubai Camel Jockeys. UNICEF. Dec. 2006. 11 Nov. 2007 <http://www.dubaicameljockeys.org/ms/ms_doc39.asp>.

R is for Rwanda

- Asiimwe, Arthur "Rwandan genocide orphans fend for selves". Mar. 2004. 26. Jan. 2008 <http://www.alertnet.org/thefacts/reliefresources/108046909955.htm>.
- King, Noel E. "Rights-Rwanda: Children of the Genocide Struggle to Cope". Inter Press Service News Agency. Jan. 2007. 27 Jan. 2008 <http://ipsnews.net/print.asp?idnews=40769>.
- McGreal, Chris "A pearl in Rwanda's genocide horror". Guardian Unlimited. Dec. 2001. 26 Jan. 2008 <http://www.guardian.co.uk/society/2001/dec/05/christmasappeal/print>.
- "Rwandan women surviving genocide now face AIDS". Afrol News. Apr. 2004. 26 Jan. 2008 <http://www.afrol.com/articles/12056>.

S is for Sudan

- "80 Sudan: Now or Never in Darfur–Africa Report." International Crisis Group. May 2004. 27 Dec. 2007 <http://www.crisisgroup.org/home/index.cfm?1=1&id=2765>.
- Hampson, Rick."Darfur crisis has activist 'angry' all the time." USA TODAY. Mar. 2007. 27 Dec. 2007 <http://www.usatoday.com/news/nation/2007-03-19-darfur-activist_N.htm>.
- Ismail, Omer and John Prendergast. "A race against time in Eastern Chad." Enough Project. Nov. 2007 <http://www.enoughproject.org>.
- Mulama, Joyce. "CHALLENGES 2006-2007: Darfur in Crisis, Still." Inter Press Service Agency Nairobi. Dec. 2006. 27 Dec. 2007 <http://ipsnews.net/print.asp?idnews=35966>.
- Prendergast, John and Adam O'Brien. "A Diplomatic Surge for Northern Uganda." ENOUGH Strategy Briefing #9. Enough Project. Dec. 2007 <http://www.enoughproject.org>.
- "Susan Atto, Sudan 'I Believe there is nobody in the world that can help me." IRIN UN-OCHA Integrated Regional Information Networks. Oct. 2006. 27 Dec. 2007 <http://www.irinnews.org/Report.aspx?ReportId=61267>.
- Thomas-Jensen, Colin and John Prendergast. "A Strategy for Success in Sirte ENOUGH Strategy Paper #10." Enough Project. Nov. 2007 <http://www.enoughproject.org>.

T is for Tibet

- "Annual Report 2006: Human Rights Situation in Tibet." Tibetan Centre for Human Rights and Democracy. Mar. 2007. 10 Jan. 2008 <http://www.tchrd.org/press/2007/pr20070302.html>.
- Kulantzick, Joshua. "The End of Tibet." Rolling Stone. Feb. 2007. 22 Mar. 2007 <http://www.rollingstone.com/news/story/13247913/the_end_of_tibet>.
- "The Panchan Lama." International Campaign for Tibet. 28 Dec. 2007 <http://www.savetibet.org/campaigns/pl/index.php>.
- "Tibet–End Torture in Tibet." International Campaign for Tibet. 10 Jan. 2008 <http://www.savetibet.org/campaigns/political prisoners/index.php>.
- "Tibet–The Issues." International Campaign for Tibet. 10 Jan. 2008 <http://www.savetibet.org/tibet/index.php>.

U for Uganda

- Anwar, Yasmin. "Damning Report on Uganda War Crimes." UC Berkley Press Release. June. 2007. 2 Dec. 2007 <http://www.berkeley.edu/news/media/releases/2007/06/15_Lra.shtml>.
- "Caution, "Breaking it Down–Children Soldiers Worldwide." Children with Guns. Jan. 2007. 2 Dec. 2007 <http://childrenwithguns.blogspot.com/2007/01/breaking-it-down-children-soldiers_22.html>.
- "Children at War–The Crisis in Northern Uganda." World Vision–Building a better world for children. 2 Dec. 2007 <http://www.worldvision.org/worldvision/wvususfo.nsf/stable/globalissues_uganda>.
- "Plight of Ugandan Child Soldiers reveals overall neglect of children's rights." UN News Centre. Dec. 2004. 2 Dec. 2007 <http://www.un.org/apps/news/story.asp?NewsID=12903&Cr=children&Cr1=>.
- Shelburne, Elizabeth. "Students bring visibility to plight of Ugandan Kids." The Boston Globe. International Reporting Project. 2006. 2 Dec. 2008 <http://www.
- journalismfellowships.org/stories/uganda/uganda_students.htm>.
- Yakubu, Amina . "G.R. Response to Uganda's Plight." Chimes. Oct. 2005. 2 Dec. 2007 <http://www-stu.calvin.edu/chimes/article.php>.

V is for Vietnam

- Brass, Dr. Martin. "The Modern Scourge of Sex Slavery." Soldier of Fortune Magazine. Sept. 2004. 27 Dec. 2007 <http://www.military.com/NewContent/0,13190,SOF_Index,00.html>.
- Lam, Andrew. "In the World of Human Trafficking, Vietnam Remains a supply Country." New America Media. Pacific News Service. July 2005. 27 Dec. 2007 <http://news.ncmonline.com/news/view_article.html?article_id=5eb46622209f2d8d0ebca1c116b2c11d>.
- Lên Đuong. "The approach is unchanging: 'You want young girl, little girl?'" Sunday Telegraph. Sept. 2002. 27 Dec.2007 <http://lenduong.net/spip.php?article7761>.

- McClelland, Susan. “Child-Sex Trade Thriving in Cambodia.” UN Reporting. Nov. 2003. 27 Dec. 2007 <http://www.thecanadianencyclopedia.com/index.cfm?PgNm=TCE&Params =M1ARTM0012537>.

W is for Western Sahara

- Frank Ruddy, US Ambassador (ret.), “Western Sahara, Africa’s Last Colony, World Affairs Council, Alaska, Juneau, October 31,2007 & Alaska, Anchorage November 2, 2007.” Posted Norwegian Support Committee for Western Sahara. Nov. 2007. 20 Jan. 2008 <http://groups.yahoo.com/group/Sahara-Update/message/1983>.
- Tom C. Varghese. “Polisario losing patience.” Global Affairs Issue 7. Posted Norwegian Support Committee for Western Sahara. Jan. 2008. 20 Jan. 2008 <http://groups.yahoo. com/group/Sahara-Update/message/2006>.
- “Support for the Sahrawi people’s right to Independence.” Norwegian Centre Party. Posted Norwegian Support Committee for Western Sahara. Jan. 2008. 20 Jan. 2008 <http:// groups.yahoo.com/group/Sahara-Update/message/2004>.
- Williams, Ian. “Practicing what you preach.” Guardian Unlimited. Posted Norwegian Support Committee for Western Sahara. Jan. 2008. 20 Jan. 2008 <http://groups.yahoo.com/ group/Sahara-Update/message/2009>.

Y is for Yemen

- al-Jarady, Eman.“Youth call upon parents, government to curtail child labor.” Yemen Observer. Jan. 2008. 19 Jan. 2008 <http://www.yobserver.com/news-varieties/ printer-10013481.html>.
- Ringer, Kandy. “Yemen’s Child Labor on the Rise Due to Deteriorated Economic Situation.” BBS News. IRIN. Sept. 2007. 19 Jan. 2008 <http://bbsnews.net/article. php/20070904104112201/print>.
- “Yemen: Trafficked children could become terrorists, specialists warn.” (IRIN) UN-OCHA Integrated Regional Information Networks. Feb. 2007. 8 Mar. 2007 <http://www. irinnews.org/PrintReport.aspx?ReportId=69922>.
- “Zaid Abdullah, Yemen, I live from hand to mouth.” IRIN UN-OCHA Integrated Regional Information Networks. Feb. 2007. 8 Feb. 2007 <http://www.irinnews.org/ PrintReport.aspx?ReportId=70271>.

Z is for Zimbabwe

- “God Hears The Cry Of The Oppressed. “ Sokwanele. April 2007. 2 Jan. 2008. <http://www.sokwanele.com/articles/sokwanele/godhearsthecries_6April2007.html>.
- “Lest we forget: The catastrophic impact of the deepening crisis on Zimbabwe’s children.” Sokwanele. Nov. 2007. 2 Jan. 2008. <http://www.sokwanele.com/articles/ lestweforgetzimbabweschildren_28112007.html>.
- “Pillage and Patronage: Human rights abuses in Zimbabwe’s informal gold mining sector.” Sokwanele. Jan 2007. 2 Jan. 2008. <http://www.sokwanele.com/articles/sokwanele/ pillage_and_patronage_27jan2007.html>.
- “Talkin’ about a revolution.” Sokwanele. Mar. 2007. 2 Jan. 2008, <http://www.sokwanele.com/articles/sokwanele/talkinaboutarevolution_23march2007.html>.
- “’The silent cries of the little ones’ Zimbabwe’s under-fives cry out for justice.” Sokwanele. Apr. 2006. 2 Jan. 2008. <http://www.sokwanele.com/articles/sokwanele/thesilentcrieso fthelittleones_10april2006.html>.
- “Zimbabwe’s forgotten children.” UNICEF – Press Center. 2 Jan. 2008. <http://www.unicef.org/media/media_25617.html>.

Additional Thanks:

I’d like to thank those who helped with the tedious job of putting these references together. Thank you Brielle, O’Brien, Samantha and Felicia. A huge thanks to you Brock for meticulously helping me see to the details.

Peace

Freedom

Equality

Hope...

For a Better

World.

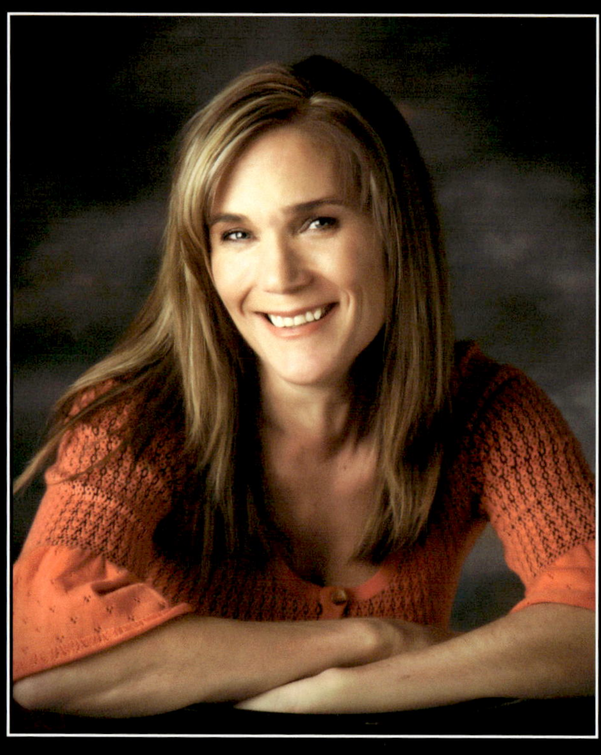

The first portrait Caryn West created was a life-size drawing of Sammy Davis Jr. to accompany a book report about his autobiography, *Yes I Can*. The portrait was done in crayon, and she was only nine years old.

Though she attended the Pasadena Art Center College of Design, most of Caryn's abilities are self-taught. Over the years she has experimented with a variety of mediums, amassing expertise in acrylic painting and graphic design while developing an acute sense of color and the ability to tell a story.

Caryn's work has been primarily in the commercial arena but her passion is working on humanitarian projects, where she can use her artistic talent and creativity to highlight global issues.

In 2006, Caryn conceived *The Trouble with the Alphabet*. Since then, her efforts have been focused on bringing her collective experience together in a project that gives full expression to her range of creativity and allows her to say, "*Yes I Can*" make a difference. Currently she lives in Colorado with her husband Brock and their three children, Felicia, Blaze and Cruz.